The Klopp 100
A Modern Liverpool Love Affair

COMPILED BY CHRIS McLOUGHLIN & ROY GILFOYLE

Reach Sport

Copyright © Liverpool Football Club

The right of Liverpool Football Club to be identified as the owner of this work has been asserted in accordance with the Copyright, Designs and Patents Act, 1988. All Rights Reserved. No part of this publication may be reproduced, stored in a retrieval system, or transmitted in any form, or by any means, electronic, mechanical, photocopying, recording or otherwise without the prior permission in writing of the copyright holders, nor be otherwise circulated in any form of binding or cover other than in which it is published and without a similar condition being imposed on the subsequent publisher.

Hardback edition first published in Great Britain in 2022
www.reachsport.com
@reach_sport
Reach Sport is a part of Reach PLC Ltd, 5 St Paul's Square, Liverpool, L3 9SJ
One Canada Square, Canary Wharf, London, E15 5AP

Hardback ISBN: 9781914197451
Photographic acknowledgements:
Liverpool FC Getty Images, Mirrorpix, PA, Alamy
Design: Rick Cooke, Lee Ashun
Writers: Chris McLoughlin, Roy Gilfoyle
Cover: Rick Cooke

Some facts and statistics from lfchistory.net

Printed and bound by Bell & Bain Limited

I FEEL FINE

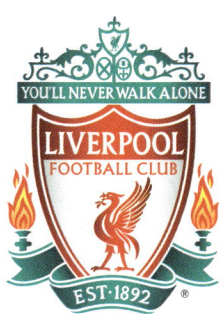

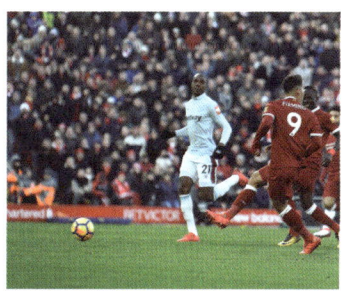

The Klopp 100

One hundred of the most striking memories, matches and aspects of Jürgen Klopp's reign as Liverpool FC manager so far. While this century of entries is not intended to be comprehensive, it brings together a collection of what makes the connection between the holy trinity of the club, the manager and the fans so strong.

I FEEL FINE

A CELEBRATION OF A MODERN LIVERPOOL LOVE AFFAIR

We both grew up as Liverpool FC supporters in the 1980s.

Well I say supporters, it was more like Liverpool FC obsessives. We didn't know each other – our paths first crossed in 2000 when we worked on the Liverpool ECHO sports desk – but it quickly became clear that our lives had always revolved around the same football club. The football club your life revolves around too.

Coincidentally, our first Anfield matches were against Newcastle – one in 1985 and the other in 1987 – yet it feels like we have lived through the eras that preceded Joe Fagan and Sir Kenny Dalglish's stints in the dugout. Why? Because of The Official History of Liverpool FC VHS.

There is an endless supply of Liverpool FC footage now. You could spend six months on LFCTV and YouTube and still not get through every game, goal or interview, but back in the 1980s seeing the Reds on the telly was rare.

One live match was shown per weekend, industrial action meant some Liverpool games were never filmed and when the BBC lost the rights to league football in 1988 there wasn't even Match of the Day on a Saturday night, with ITV often only showing goals from featured games on news bulletins or on The Saint & Greavsie Show the following Saturday morning.

So for Liverpool-mad kids like ourselves, The Official History of Liverpool FC – produced by the BBC, narrated by John Motson and with Dalglish on the cover sleeve in a classic Crown Paints kit – was manna from heaven.

Between us we watched that video so often that we can still recite plenty of it now from the plummy-voiced Panorama reporter standing in front of the Kop in the 1960s to various pieces of commentary. "And here comes Avi Cohen….oh I say, at the same end he's got one back!"

But there was one man, above all, who appeared on that VHS and absolutely captivated both of us. Bill Shankly.

It was his aura. His accent. His words. His confidence. The way in which he was idolised

to the point where some Liverpool supporters would bow at his feet. It was how he sat tapping the Football League trophy while drumming it into us that it was "our bread and butter," like a headmaster setting the rules.

Shankly died in 1981, before either of us were really old enough to appreciate him, but here he was on VHS as a living, breathing, messiah; a leader who walked around the Anfield pitch in his bright-coloured shirt and dapper suit with his arms aloft as he received adulation like none other. It was awesome.

If ever time machines become a reality, that's where we're both going first: Shankly's Anfield. But now isn't the time to be going back to the past because in the present we've got the Shankly of our generation managing Liverpool FC.

Jürgen Klopp is our modern-day equivalent. He isn't Shankly, nor should he be. If you're not a first-rate version of yourself you're a second-rate manager, but in terms of having a Liverpool boss with the power to harness the Anfield crowd, to think in the same way as so many of us, to build teams that combine hard work, quality, emotion and belief, then Klopp is the perfect fit.

He has charisma, confidence, family values and a sense of humour, but also a steely edge and a fierce winning mentality. He has built a collective spirit where every man gives his all on the pitch and the Anfield crowd gives their all off it.

He has also delivered the two trophies all Liverpool followers crave the most – the European Cup and the Premier League.

Add the FA Cup, League Cup, UEFA Super Cup, FIFA Club World Cup and Community Shield to that haul and Klopp is the only Liverpool manager to have completed such a collection – seven different trophies in seven seasons.

So when the Reds were bidding for a historic quadruple of trophies in 2021/22, when Klopp thankfully signed a new long-term contract to stay as Liverpool FC manager and when the ear worm that is the 'I'm in love with him and I feel

> **'JÜRGEN KLOPP ISN'T SHANKLY, NOR SHOULD HE BE. BUT IN TERMS OF THE POWER TO HARNESS THE ANFIELD CROWD, AND BUILDING TEAMS THAT COMBINE HARD WORK, QUALITY, EMOTION AND BELIEF, KLOPP IS THE PERFECT FIT'**

fine' chant started living rent free in our heads, we had one of those 'Jürgen must have given us a hundred boss memories by now' conversations with our executive editor and fellow Red, Paul Dove.

From that seed grew this book – a celebration of a modern Liverpool love affair to mark the seventh anniversary of Jürgen Klopp's appointment as LFC manager.

I Feel Fine is 100 moments, memories and characteristics of the Jürgen Klopp era. It's not just about the Liverpool manager, but Liverpool players, Liverpool coaches and Liverpool supporters. It isn't exhaustive either, rather a collection of 100 things that have given us inspiration, joy and a sense of belonging to the greatest club in the world.

This book is a celebration of the unique bond Kopites have with Jürgen Klopp, a relationship that feels as special and as powerful to us as we can only imagine it felt to Kopites when Bill Shankly was leading Liverpool Football Club.

Quite simply, it was written because we're so glad that Jürgen is a Red…

Chris McLoughlin & Roy Gilfoyle

I FEEL FINE

BOOM!

Four letters that form a short onomatopoeic word that so perfectly sums up our boss and the impact he's had on Liverpool Football Club. 'Boom' could be the effect Jürgen Klopp had on everyone at the club. 'Boom' could be the dynamic way his team attacks opponents. 'Boom' could be the noise inside Anfield when watching Klopp's men go for the jugular. The popular gif of Klopp saying 'Boom!' comes from a post-match interview in 2016. The Reds had just beaten Manchester City 3-0 at Anfield in the same season they won 4-1 at the Etihad, but coming off the back of a League Cup final defeat to City three days earlier, the home win was particularly pleasing. Only a few months into the job, Klopp was already captivating Reds supporters and Premier League football fans generally – and he always knows the right words to sum up a performance…

I FEEL FINE

"IT WAS OUR BEST HOME GAME *[IN HIS TIME SO FAR AS LIVERPOOL MANAGER]*. THE BEST WORD I CAN SAY THAT CAN DESCRIBE THIS IS…

BOOM!

WOAH, WHAT WAS THIS?!"

"IT'S NOT IMPORTANT WHAT PEOPLE SAID WHEN YOU COME IN, BUT WHAT THEY SAY WHEN YOU LEAVE. IF WE WANT, THIS COULD BE A SPECIAL DAY"

I FEEL FINE

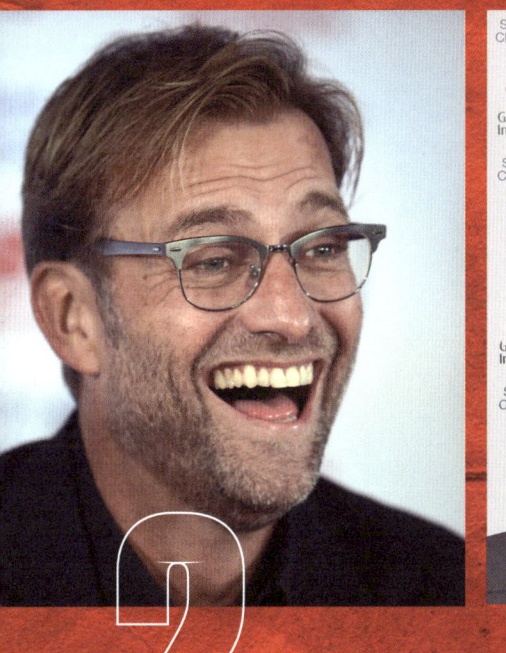

2 THE 'NORMAL ONE'

Liverpool was made for Jürgen Klopp and Jürgen Klopp was made for Liverpool – that much was evident right from the start. The arrival of a new manager usually brings an air of optimism and the hope that the new man can bring better results than his immediate predecessor – but it's fair to say that the then 48-year-old said all the right things in his opening press conference as Liverpool manager in 2015. He matched humility ("I am the normal one") with confidence ("If we sit here in four years, I think we win a title, I'm pretty sure") – and added a splash of humour. Several years of incredible football, fantastic signings and trophy success later, the 'normal one' has proven to be anything but.

Words of wisdom – the first press conference:

"IF SOMEONE WANTS TO HELP THEY HAVE TO CHANGE FROM DOUBTER TO BELIEVER"

"I DON'T COMPARE MYSELF WITH THESE GENIUSES WITHIN THE HISTORY OF LIVERPOOL. NONE OF THESE MANAGERS SAID THEY WANTED TO BE A LEGEND WHEN THEY ARRIVED. THIS IS A GREAT CLUB BECAUSE OF MANY GOOD DECISIONS IN THE PAST"

"I'M LOOKING FORWARD TO THE INTENSITY OF FOOTBALL AND HOW THE PEOPLE LIVE FOOTBALL IN LIVERPOOL. IT'S A SPECIAL CLUB"

THE FIRST STEP

You couldn't really say Jürgen Klopp's first match as Liverpool manager was a true sign of what was to come, but there were a few hints at what we could expect in the future. The 0-0 draw with Tottenham Hotspur at White Hart Lane was less eventful than most of the matches that would follow, but a point against a talented side wasn't a bad way to start. Klopp prowled up and down the touchline and bellowed his encouragement – and maybe it was this that prompted Liverpool to produce their best running stats of the season up until that point, covering around 4km more than the next best match. And at the end of the game, Klopp showed his appreciation to his players by giving each of them a hug. The new LFC boss said: "0-0 is not my dream result, but it is okay. I am happy because I saw many good things, in the first 20 minutes we were pressing and were very aggressive. We will get stronger. There were many full-throttle moments in the game. We need to improve but after working with the players for three days I am completely satisfied."

I FEEL FINE

3

Media reaction to Klopp's first game:

JAMES PEARCE, LIVERPOOL ECHO:
'THE KLOPP EFFECT WAS EVIDENT IN THE CAPITAL. HIS APPOINTMENT HAS CLEARLY NOT ONLY GALVANISED THE FANBASE BUT ALSO THE DRESSING ROOM'

DANIEL TAYLOR, THE GUARDIAN:
'LIVERPOOL BECAME A TEAM OF ONE GOALKEEPER AND 10 JAMES MILNERS AND KLOPP MUST HAVE BEEN ENCOURAGED BY THE SPEED AT WHICH HIS CHANGES HAVE BEEN IMPLEMENTED'

PAUL HAYWARD, THE TELEGRAPH:
'NOBODY WANTS TO HEAR IT, BUT IT WILL TAKE TWO YEARS OR MORE TO RAISE THE QUALITY OF THIS SQUAD TO WHERE IT NEEDS TO BE. BUT THIS WAS A "COOL" ENOUGH BEGINNING'

MICHAEL COX, ESPN:
'THE MOST NOTABLE ASPECT OF LIVERPOOL'S PERFORMANCE WAS THE INTENSE PRESSING. IT WASN'T TOTAL PRESSING THAT SHUT DOWN TOTTENHAM ALL OVER THE PITCH BUT WHEN SPURS ATTEMPTED TO PLAY THE BALL INTO THE MIDFIELD ZONE, LIVERPOOL SPRUNG INTO LIFE QUICKLY'

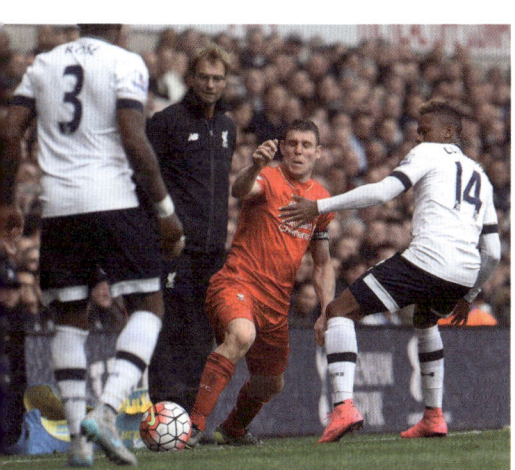

4

A SPECIAL DRAW

It was one of the first clear examples of how Jürgen Klopp was building the sacred bond between players, manager and fans – and it came after a draw at home to a mid-table team. The visitors were West Brom and the mid-December match wasn't one that would have stood out on that day's fixture list. But the game threw up some difficulties for the Reds. Having taken the

lead through Jordan Henderson, Tony Pulis' side scored from two set-pieces and deep into time added on, the Reds were 2-1 down. Divock Origi – so often a man who likes late drama – struck from distance and his deflected effort earned a point. Apart from the defensive lapses, Klopp was happy with the performance, and he was equally happy with how the crowd stayed with the players, saying it was the best atmosphere he'd experienced in his two months in charge. So, he and his team showed their appreciation by walking towards the Kop and raising their arms to a raucous reception. The outside world may have mocked what they considered to be over-celebrating a home draw, but the connection was strengthening and an empire was slowly building.

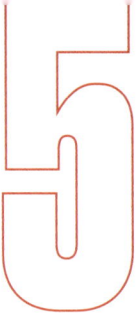

Premier League
23 January 2016

Norwich 4
Mbokani (29)
Naismith (40)
Hoolahan (53)
Bassong (90)

Liverpool 5
Firmino (18, 63)
Henderson (55)
Milner (74)
Lallana (90+5)

It was one of the more bizarre matches Liverpool have been involved in during Jürgen Klopp's reign and it came just a few months after his appointment. The setting was Carrow Road and the inconsistent Reds were taking on a Norwich City side equally capable of scoring goals – but conceding them in large volumes too. It was a game the Redmen seemed to have to win several times over. Bobby Firmino gave the Reds the lead but Dieumerci Mbokani and Steven Naismith turned the match on its head and Wes Hoolahan stretched Norwich's lead to 3-1 on 53 minutes. Liverpool kicked into life with Jordan Henderson sweeping home, and Firmino equalised with his second goal of the afternoon, before James Milner made it 4-3. The fun wasn't over. Sebastien Bassong looked to have earned the home side a point in the 90th minute but a manic finish was rounded off when Adam Lallana's bouncing effort evaded everyone in a crowded box to make it 5-4. In the wild celebrations that followed, Klopp himself joined the ecstatic players and in the mayhem Christian Benteke knocked his manager's glasses off his face and broke them. A year later, after Benteke had moved on, Klopp looked back at the game and joked: "They were absolutely broken! In the picture I have them in my hands. It was Christian Benteke who did it. So don't kill my glasses or otherwise you will be sold!"

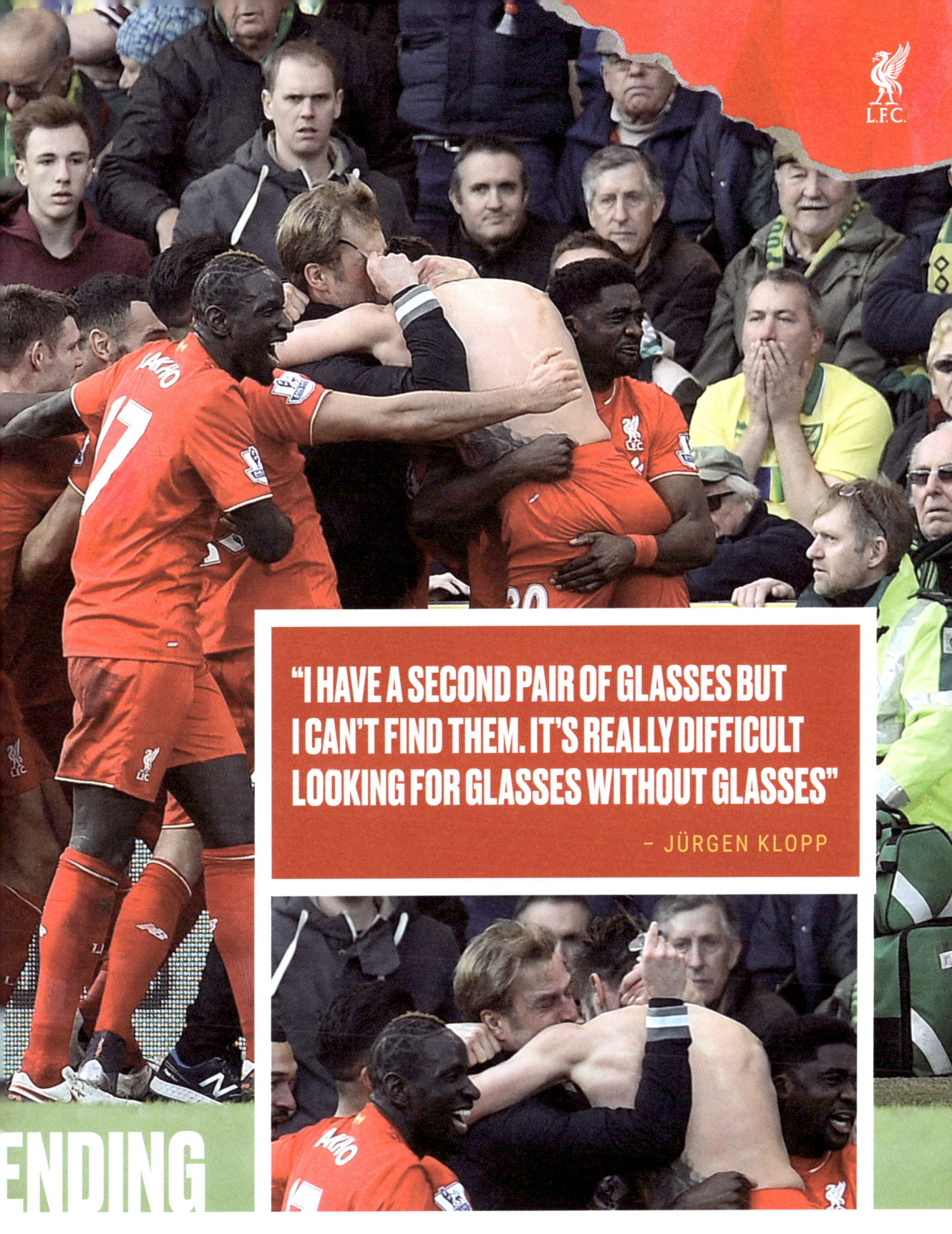

"I HAVE A SECOND PAIR OF GLASSES BUT I CAN'T FIND THEM. IT'S REALLY DIFFICULT LOOKING FOR GLASSES WITHOUT GLASSES"

– JÜRGEN KLOPP

6
SPOT ON

The first penalty shoot-out of the Jürgen Klopp era sent Liverpool to Wembley with an unlikely hero converting the final kick. The Reds faced Stoke in a two-legged League Cup semi-final in January 2016 and, having secured a 1-0 win at the Britannia Stadium thanks to Jordon Ibe's left-footed strike, they were strong favourites to finish off the job. Mark Hughes' stubborn side made life very difficult though and Marko Arnautovic scored the only goal of the second leg, so a place in the final would be decided by penalties. Both sides converted four of their original five and it was 5-5 when Simon Mignolet made an excellent save from Marc Muniesa. Future Stoke midfielder Joe Allen slotted the ball into the top right corner to send Liverpool to a first cup final under Klopp's management. Many more would follow.

I FEEL FINE

> **The Reds have won 19 out of 26 penalty shoot-outs they have contested throughout their history.
> This 6-5 victory on penalties in 2016 meant Liverpool had won an impressive 14 out of 17 at this point**

KNOCKING UNITED OUT

It's remarkable really that English football's two biggest clubs have only ever faced each other once – over two legs – in European competition. It's even more remarkable that when that occasion finally arrived, it came in UEFA's second-tier competition, the Europa League, in 2016. Neither team was at the peak of its powers at the time as Jürgen Klopp was still only five months into his time at Liverpool while the Red Devils were inconsistent in the post-Alex Ferguson era. But this was a historic occasion and a round of 16 tie both teams desperately wanted to win. Much of the hard work was done in a first leg the Reds completely dominated. David de Gea had to be on top form at Anfield to keep Klopp's men to just a 2-0 victory courtesy of a Daniel Sturridge penalty and a simple finish from Bobby Firmino. United struck first in the return leg with an Anthony Martial penalty, but a magical goal from Philippe Coutinho, who skipped down the left before producing a cute near-post finish, equalised on the night and ended the home side's momentum. First blood in European competition between these two giants went to the Reds.

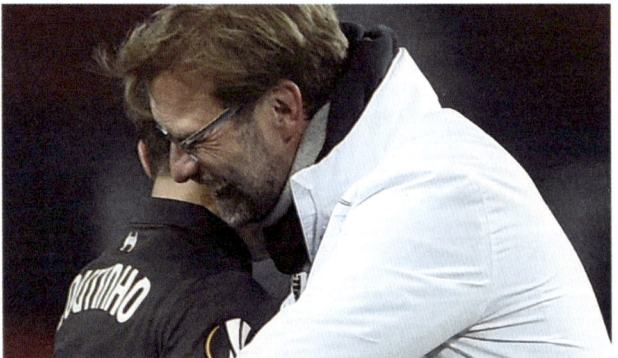

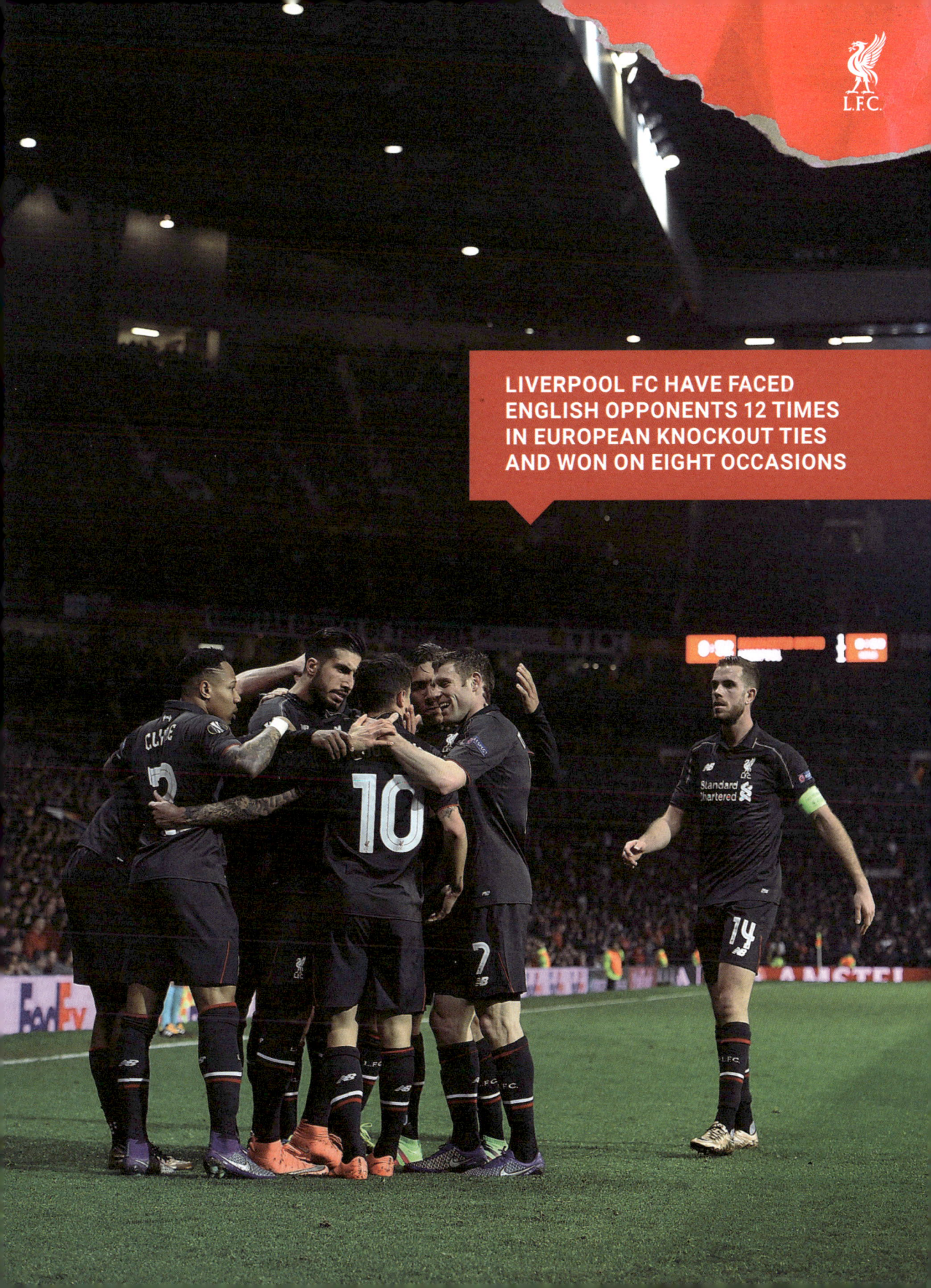

LIVERPOOL FC HAVE FACED ENGLISH OPPONENTS 12 TIMES IN EUROPEAN KNOCKOUT TIES AND WON ON EIGHT OCCASIONS

I FEEL FINE

8 DORTMUND FIGHTBACK

Jürgen Klopp's first European campaign as Reds boss was characteristically eventful – even if the Europa League group stage was already up and running by the time he arrived. The Reds finished top of a group containing Sion, Rubin Kazan and Bordeaux before a single goal saw off Augsburg at the round of 16 stage. There followed the first-ever meeting between the Reds and Manchester United in European competition, the despatching of Villarreal in the semi-finals before a topsy-turvy final against Sevilla, which ended in defeat. The most memorable contest had to be the quarter-final against Klopp's former club Borussia Dortmund. A 1-1 draw in Germany set Anfield up for a massive night against a team containing the class of Marco Reus, Henrikh Mkhitaryan and Pierre-Emerick Aubameyang among others. Within 10 minutes Mkhitaryan and Aubameyang had given Thomas Tuchel's men a commanding lead. Though Divock Origi pulled a goal back at the start of the second half, Reus made it 3-1 on the night. To some clubs that would have been a killer blow. For Liverpool, it's the kind of challenge the Kop relishes. Philippe Coutinho scored from outside the box before Mamadou Sakho nodded in from a corner to level and leave Dortmund clinging on to an away goals advantage. The Reds pushed for a winner and it arrived in added time as Dejan Lovren powered in a header then slid into the corner as pandemonium broke out. It was the first really magical European night at Anfield for Klopp. It wouldn't be the last.

I FEEL FINE

**Europa League quarter-final first leg
7 April 2016**

B Dortmund 1
Hummels (48)

Liverpool 1
Origi (36)

**Europa League quarter-final second leg
14 April 2016**

Liverpool 4
Origi (48)
Coutinho (66)
Sakho (78)
Lovren (90+1)

B Dortmund 3
Mkhitaryan (5)
Aubameyang (9)
Reus (57)

(Liverpool win 5-4 on aggregate)

I FEEL FINE

I FEEL FINE

9
SUBMARINE SINKS

Liverpool have only played Villarreal four times in European competition and each match has come at the semi-final stage. The first meeting came in the last four of the Europa League in 2016. After seeing off a team in bright yellow (Borussia Dortmund) in the previous round, Liverpool succumbed 1-0 to the Yellow Submarine in the first leg at El Madrigal, setting up a big night at Anfield. There was a turbo-charged atmosphere for the second leg, not only to help the team turn around the deficit on the pitch, but because of the recent inquiry verdict of 'unlawfully killed' for the 96 victims of the Hillsborough disaster. After Liverpool supporters had displayed a mosaic reading 'The Greatest Football Family', the Reds made a fast start and a Bruno Soriano own goal levelled the tie. Daniel Sturridge put Jürgen Klopp's men ahead before Adam Lallana's goal confirmed a place in the final against Sevilla, nine years after the club's last European showpiece. Fast forward six years and Villarreal, this time under the guidance of Unai Emery, stood between the Reds and a place in the 2022 Champions League final. The home leg came first this time and Liverpool were very good value for their 2-0 win, the goals coming from an Pervis Estupinan own goal and Sadio Mane. The Villarreal fans were fired up for the return leg in soggy Spain, and their team wiped out the Reds' lead by half-time. Fabinho calmed Liverpool nerves before Luis Diaz and Mane gave the final 5-2 aggregate scoreline a more comfortable feel to send the Redmen to Paris.

I FEEL FINE

I FEEL FINE

Europa League semi-final first leg
28 April 2016

Villarreal 1
Liverpool 0
Lopez (90)

Europa League semi-final second leg
5 May 2016

Liverpool 3   **Villarreal 0**
Soriano (7 og)
Sturridge (63)
Lallana (81)

(Liverpool win 3-1 on aggregate)

Champions League semi-final first leg
27 April 2022

Liverpool 2   **Villarreal 0**
Estupinan (53 og)
Mane (55)

Champions League semi-final second leg
3 May 2022

Villarreal 2   **Liverpool 3**
Dia (3)   Fabinho (62)
Coquelin (41)   Diaz (67)
                     Mane (74)

(Liverpool win 5-2 on aggregate)

10
AN EARLY STATEMENT

Big things were expected as Liverpool kicked off what would be Jürgen Klopp's first full season as boss. The club had been active in the transfer market over the summer, bringing in Sadio Mane and Georginio Wijnaldum, as well as Joel Matip on a free transfer. All three would become key players in future successes, but for now fans were most keen to see how the Senegalese forward would contribute to the Reds' attacking play. It was an unsettled start for the new-look line-up as Theo Walcott gave Arsenal the lead only a minute after having his penalty saved by Simon Mignolet. But just before half-time, an established star in Philippe Coutinho produced a sublime free-kick to level matters, and after the break Klopp's men went up a gear. Adam Lallana finished off a great team move before Coutinho made it 3-1. The Arsenal fans were already showing their displeasure by the time Mane produced some individual magic to burn down the right, cut in on his left and find the far top corner, celebrating by jumping on his manager's back. The Gunners made it a nervy finish as Alex Oxlade-Chamberlain and Calum Chambers brought it back to 4-3 – but the Reds held on and began a season that would be a step in the right direction.

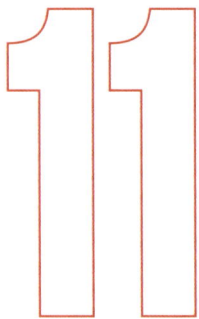

11

GROWTH OF THE GROUND

There has been significant change on the pitch during Jürgen Klopp's period in charge at Anfield, but there has been a lot of change off it too. Less than a year after becoming manager, Klopp, the players, and the fans lucky enough to get tickets, could look up at a much larger and greatly improved Main Stand. Leicester City were the visitors the first time the expanded stand was in use for a Premier League match and the extra 8,500 supporters were treated to a 4-1 win in September 2016. So high it can be seen from across the Mersey and beyond, the Main Stand redevelopment work included the addition of 96 Avenue (renamed 97 Avenue since the death of 97th Hillsborough victim Andrew Devine), a smart boulevard alongside the stand that encompasses the Hillsborough Memorial, benches remembering the feats of some of the Reds' greatest players, and a walkway of fans' Anfield Forever stones. And the expansion continues. Klopp attended the ground-breaking ceremony as work began on improving the Anfield Road stand in 2021, a project that will raise the capacity at the stadium to over 60,000 by the time the 2023/24 season begins.

I FEEL FINE

12 LATE SHOW

Derby matches are always important. If you're from a 'mixed' family or community that contains both Liverpudlians and Evertonians, the result can be the difference between having bragging rights or hiding for a few weeks until the heat dies down. The intensity of that desire to win doubles or triples if the derby match falls just before Christmas – a time when 'mixed' gatherings are inevitable. Maybe that's why Sadio Mane's added-time winner at Goodison Park on 19 December 2016 felt so special and was even immortalised in song. In the 94th minute Daniel Sturridge dribbled across the edge of the box before directing a shot against the post. Mane reacted quickest to poke in from five yards – and a new chant, to the tune of Merry Christmas Everyone by Shakin' Stevens, was born...

I FEEL FINE

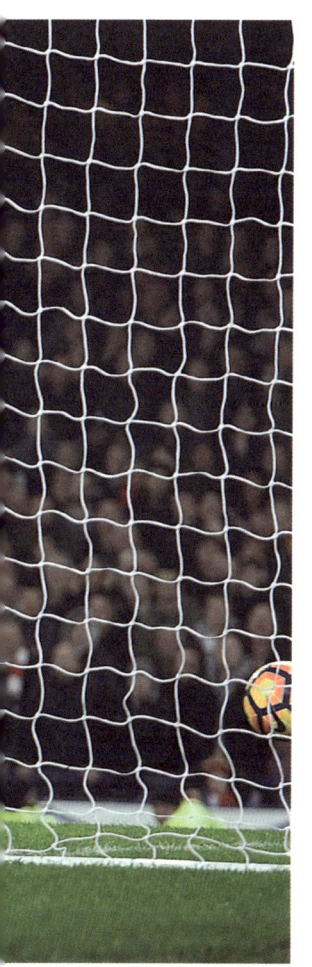

MANE SCORING, ALL AROUND US, KOPITES SINGING, HAVING FUN, IT'S THE SEASON, LOVE AND UNDERSTANDING, MERRY CHRISTMAS, EVERTON!

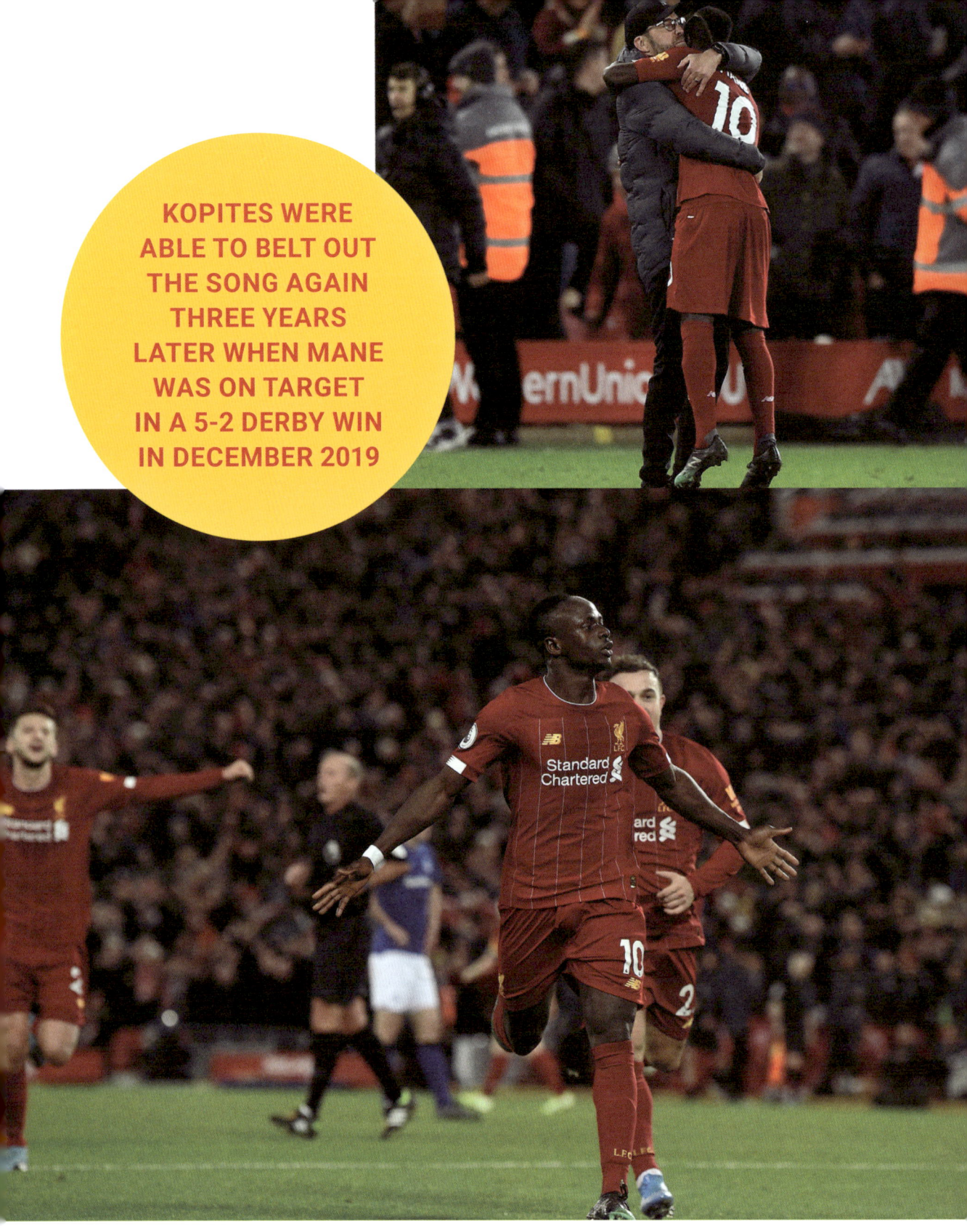

KOPITES WERE ABLE TO BELT OUT THE SONG AGAIN THREE YEARS LATER WHEN MANE WAS ON TARGET IN A 5-2 DERBY WIN IN DECEMBER 2019

WITH THREE DECEMBER DERBY GOALS OF HIS OWN, KOPITES HAVE BEEN KNOWN TO SUBSTITUTE MANE'S NAME IN THE 'MERRY CHRISTMAS EVERYONE' LYRICS WITH DIVOCK ORIGI'S

13

OVERHEAD POWER

It was a thing of beauty, totally out of context with most other aspects of a drab game. It was a goal worth the admission fee on its own – which was lucky because there wasn't much else for a neutral to savour as the Reds claimed a 1-0 win against Watford at Vicarage Road. With the clock having ticked past 45 minutes at the end of an uneventful half, Lucas picked up the ball in midfield and spotted German midfielder Emre Can venturing into the box. The Brazilian's lofted pass was a good one, but he probably didn't expect it to go down as a goal assist. Can turned it into one. He twisted his body and produced one of the greatest overhead kicks you'll ever see. Heurelho Gomes tried to save it, but he had no chance. Team-mate Adam Lallana said: "It was a worldy goal and worthy of winning any game." He wasn't wrong and Emre's effort won the 2016/17 BBC Match of the Day Goal of the Season award.

14
TENSE BUT TRIUMPHANT

A promising first full season at Liverpool had seen Jürgen Klopp lead his troops to fourth place with one game to go, but with Arsenal breathing down their necks. No-one could argue that there had been significant improvement, but the Reds needed tangible reward to show for their efforts – and set them up for an even more prosperous 2017/18 season. And the prospect of Champions League football returning to Anfield would help attract and retain talented players. Fans lined the streets to greet the arrival of the team bus before a game against Middlesbrough that the Reds had to win to guarantee a top-four finish. The first half was tense as half-chances came and went and the crowd looked on anxiously before the deadlock was broken on the stroke of half-time. Gini Wijnaldum ended his first season at the club with a magnificent goal at the Kop end and the Reds put the result beyond doubt with a fast start to the second period. Philippe Coutinho threaded in a wonderful free-kick to double the lead before a tidy left-footed finish from Adam Lallana completed the scoring. Arsenal won too, but Liverpool's victory secured Champions League qualification for only the second time in eight seasons. Klopp's Redmen were on the rise.

"THE BOYS PLAYED SOME FANTASTIC FOOTBALL. I'M REALLY LOOKING FORWARD TO NEXT SEASON. I THINK WE HAVE CREATED A WONDERFUL BASE. THE BETTER YOU'RE ORGANISED, THE MORE YOU FEEL FREE TO DO SPECIAL THINGS IN OFFENCE. I'M REALLY HAPPY ABOUT THIS – WHAT A WONDERFUL DAY"

– JÜRGEN KLOPP

15 SIGN RIGHT HERE...

Recruitment. It's a word that is often used in relation to teams that have either done really well or really badly in recent seasons. With Liverpool FC it is a word that has positive associations. In short: Liverpool do recruitment well. While we'd all love to see a team packed with academy-produced stars, when you're operating at an elite level, the net has to be cast wider – and the attention to detail required to bring in the right players for the right price means Liverpool usually get their recruitment right. In recent years sporting director Michael Edwards has received a lot of credit for helping Jürgen Klopp bring in and move on the right players at the right time, with Julian Ward now assuming the role. Sadio Mane was the first big success in the transfer market under Klopp in 2016 with Joel Matip and Gini Wijnaldum also joining that summer. Mo Salah arrived a year later and was an instant success while Andy Robertson was a bargain signing shortly after. 2018 saw the arrival of Virgil van Dijk, Alisson, Naby Keita and Fabinho and the Reds have carried on supplementing the squad with both high-profile and under-the-radar acquisitions ever since, including Thiago, Kostas Tsimikas, Diogo Jota and Ibou Kontae. If Luis Diaz, Fabio Carvalho and Darwin Nunez do anywhere near as well as the other major signings the Reds have made in the Klopp era, Liverpool's reputation for shrewd recruitment will continue to grow.

THIS IS ANFIELD

"I WILL GIVE 100 PER CENT AND GIVE EVERYTHING FOR THE CLUB. I REALLY WANT TO WIN SOMETHING FOR THIS CLUB"
– MO SALAH, JUNE 2017

"I'VE PLAYED AGAINST LIVERPOOL AND I'VE SEEN THEM IN LOTS OF GAMES IN THE CHAMPIONS LEAGUE, AND IT'S MY STYLE OF PLAY"

– DARWIN NUNEZ, JUNE 2022

"IT'S A REALLY EXCITING MOMENT FOR ME. TO JOIN A CLUB LIKE LIVERPOOL – THE WORLD CHAMPIONS – IS JUST UNBELIEVABLE"
– DIOGO JOTA, SEPTEMBER 2020

"THE MOST IMPORTANT THING IS THE SIZE OF THE CLUB, THE CULTURE, THE PLAYERS, THE MANAGER AND OBVIOUSLY THE FANS"
– VIRGIL VAN DIJK, JANUARY 2018

I FEEL FINE

Signings in the Klopp era

Marko Grujic	Red Star Belgrade	Jan 2016
Steven Caulker (loan)	QPR	Jan 2016
Kamil Grabara	Ruch Chorzow	Jan 2016
Sadio Mane	Southampton	Jun 2016
Loris Karius	Mainz 05	Jul 2016
Joel Matip	Free transfer	Jul 2016
Ragnar Klavan	Augsburg	Jul 2016
Alex Manninger	Free transfer	Jul 2016
Georginio Wijnaldum	Newcastle United	Jul 2016
Mohamed Salah	Roma	Jun 2017
Dominic Solanke	Chelsea	Jul 2017
Andy Robertson	Hull City	Jul 2017
Alex Oxlade-Chamberlain	Arsenal	Aug 2017
Virgil van Dijk	Southampton	Jan 2018
Naby Keita	RB Leipzig	Jul 2018
Fabinho	Monaco	Jul 2018
Xherdan Shaqiri	Stoke City	Jul 2018
Alisson Becker	Roma	Jul 2018
Sepp van den Berg	PEC Zwolle	Jun 2019
Harvey Elliott	Fulham	Jul 2019
Adrian	Free transfer	Aug 2019
Andy Lonergan	Free transfer	Aug 2019
Takumi Minamino	RB Salzburg	Jan 2020
Kostas Tsimikas	Olympiacos	Aug 2020
Thiago Alcantara	Bayern Munich	Sep 2020
Diogo Jota	Wolves	Sep 2020
Marcelo Pitaluga	Fluminense	Oct 2020
Ben Davies	Preston North End	Feb 2021
Ozan Kabak (loan)	Schalke 04	Feb 2021
Kaide Gordon	Derby County	Feb 2021
Ibrahima Konate	RB Leipzig	Jul 2021
Luis Diaz	Porto	Jan 2022
Darwin Nunez	Benfica	Jun 2022
Calvin Ramsay	Aberdeen	Jun 2022
Fabio Carvalho	Fulham	Jul 2022
Arthur Melo (loan)	Juventus	Sep 2022

"I WILL GIVE MY HEART ON THE FIELD TO MY TEAM-MATES, THE CLUB AND ALSO TO THE FANS"
– THIAGO ALCANTARA, SEPTEMBER 2020

"I'M VERY PROUD TO HAVE THE CHANCE TO PLAY ALONGSIDE MY TEAM-MATES AND TO SHARE A DRESSING ROOM WITH THEM IS A GREAT SOURCE OF PRIDE FOR ME"

– LUIS DIAZ, JANUARY 2022

I FEEL FINE

I FEEL FINE

16

AWESOME THREESOME

GOALS IN THE 2017/18 SEASON

Mohamed Salah 44
Roberto Firmino 27
Sadio Mane 20

ASSISTS IN THE 2017/18 SEASON

Roberto Firmino 16
Mohamed Salah 14
Sadio Mane 9

12 August 2017 is a significant date in the recent history of our club. It was the first time Roberto Firmino, Sadio Mane and Mohamed Salah started an official match together. And fittingly, they all scored. It was the first Premier League match of the 2017/18 season, away at Watford, and the trio gave a strong indication of what was to unfold over coming campaigns. Not only did all three get on the scoresheet in a 3-3 draw, there were a couple of assists too as Salah was brought down for the penalty that Firmino converted before the latter returned the compliment, lobbing goalkeeper Heurelho Gomes to tee up Salah from close range. Mane had earlier equalised for the Reds with a stunning finish after a superb move involving Alberto Moreno and Emre Can. One of the most lethal forward lines in English football history was up and running.

I FEEL FINE

KENNY'S STAND

In May 2017, as part of Liverpool FC's 125th anniversary celebrations, the club announced that the Centenary Stand would be renamed after Kenny Dalglish. "In Kenny Dalglish we have a person who carries such immense significance to the fabric of this club, so it feels somewhat incumbent on us to recognise this in a manner that is befitting to the man," said Fenway Sports Group principal owner John W Henry. "Kenny's contribution to Liverpool goes beyond goals scored, points amassed and silverware placed in the cabinet. His values are Liverpool's values – he represents what is best about this football club. The leadership and solace he gave to individuals, the club and city as it tried to come to terms with the trauma and tragedy of Hillsborough transcended sporting achievement. His name is synonymous with our club, with our home and the city of Liverpool. Now it will be as visible as it is palpable." The Kenny Dalglish Stand was officially unveiled on 13 October 2017, shortly after the 40th anniversary of his arrival from Celtic. "It was a huge honour, obviously, not just for myself but for the whole family," he said. "I felt a wee bit embarrassed as well because I never set out to achieve something as big as this. I just went and did my work and there are lots of other people who came here and did their work as well, but for some reason they've picked my name to put up on the stand. For us as a family, and for everybody who has helped us, it's a huge honour." The stand has since been renamed the Sir Kenny Dalglish Stand, following King Kenny's knighthood in 2018, and – quite remarkably – Jürgen Klopp's Reds went into season 2022/23 having never lost a Premier League game played in front of a crowd at Anfield since the stand was named after Dalglish.

I FEEL FINE

I FEEL FINE

18
SEVEN7H HEAVEN

In 130 years of playing football, Liverpool FC have won five matches away from home 7-0. Two were in the second division in the 1890s, one was in the FA Cup at Birmingham in 2006, and two were under Jürgen Klopp's management in the Champions League and Premier League. Both were new club records. The Reds headed to Slovenia to face NK Maribor in the 2017/18 Champions League group stage and wearing a vibrant orange change kit they took the home side apart. Roberto Firmino, Philippe Coutinho and Mo Salah (2) had the game won by half-time before Firmino again, Alex Oxlade-Chamberlain – with his first goal for LFC – and Trent Alexander-Arnold completed a rout. It was a new record away European win for Liverpool and just to show it was no fluke, the Reds ended their group stage campaign with a 7-0 Anfield success against Spartak Moscow. A Coutinho hat-trick, two for Sadio Mane, plus goals from Firmino and Salah set a new English record for the most goals in a group stage (23). Three years later, and two days after being named as 2020 FIFA Men's Coach of the Year, Klopp took Liverpool to Selhurst Park where they thrashed Crystal Palace 7-0 in the Premier League. The goals were scored by Takumi Minamino, Mane, Firmino (2), Jordan Henderson and Salah (2), but perhaps more remarkable was that seven different players – Mane, Firmino, Andy Robertson, Alexander-Arnold, Salah, Joel Matip and Oxlade-Chamberlain – supplied the assists. Sadly it was a match played behind closed doors due to the pandemic, but it sits in the record books as Liverpool's biggest top-flight away victory and only the second time the Reds had scored seven in an away league game in the top division, having won 7-1 at Derby County in 1991. Liverpool's record top-flight win at Anfield was also against Crystal Palace, a 9-0 success in 1990 that was matched by Klopp's men in 2022 when Bournemouth were beaten 9-0 with Luis Diaz (2), Firmino (2), Harvey Elliott, Alexander-Arnold, Virgil van Dijk, Fabio Carvalho and a Chris Mepham own goal making it a day to remember.

19

It was a certainty right from the very start that Virgil van Dijk and Liverpool were meant for each other – and a dream debut made that even more obvious to everyone. Having signed for the Reds only a few days earlier, the big Dutchman got to pull on the Liverpool number four jersey in a match for the first time on Friday 5 January 2018 for an FA Cup third round tie with Everton at Anfield. No nerves for Virgil though. He was calm as you like from the first whistle, stroking the ball around with precision and purpose, rarely looking flustered in his defensive duties. James Milner gave Liverpool the lead from the penalty spot in the first half, but Gylfi Sigurdsson equalised against the run of play. With six minutes to go, having watched him defend, we were able to watch him score for the first time. Alex Oxlade-Chamberlain's corner was swung in and Van Dijk leapt higher than two Everton centre-backs and Jordan Pickford to nod into an empty net. A knee-slide celebration later, the bond between fans and star signing was sealed.

I FEEL FINE

INSTANT
PACT

I FEEL FINE

SALAH'S STUNNER

"PEOPLE WATCHED THIS GAME ALL OVER THE WORLD AND THIS IS WHY – TAKE YOUR HEART, THROW IT ON THE PITCH AND PLAY LIKE THIS, BOTH TEAMS"

– JÜRGEN KLOPP

20

Manchester City were flying high at the top of the table, unbeaten in their first 22 Premier League matches of the season, when they came to Anfield in January 2018. Liverpool had just lost their most creative player, Philippe Coutinho, to Barcelona. But any thought that the loss would weaken Liverpool's attacking threat was washed away on a thrilling afternoon. Alex Oxlade-Chamberlain gave the Reds a first-half lead, but Leroy Sane levelled before the break. A breathtaking nine-minute blast in the second period really showed that the Reds were in the mood. First, Bobby Firmino shrugged off John Stones before delightfully clipping the ball over Ederson. Then Sadio Mane blasted a left-footed shot from the edge of the box into the top corner. Anfield really went wild when Ederson's panicked clearance fell to Mo Salah, who cushioned the ball then lofted it into the net from 40 yards. City showed their attacking prowess too by pulling two goals back, but the Reds had inflicted a first defeat of the season on Pep Guardiola's men. While City still went on to comfortably win the title, his stunning effort in this match was Salah's 24th goal of what would be a record-breaking season.

BOBBY'S MILESTONE MOMENTS

First LFC goal:
21.11.2015
v Manchester City (a)

First LFC hat-trick:
29.12.2018
v Arsenal (h)

100th LFC goal:
27.08.2022
v Bournemouth (h)

I FEEL FINE

"I REMEMBER THE FIRST NO-LOOK GOAL I SCORED FOR HOFFENHEIM. I ROUNDED THE GOALKEEPER AND TURNED AWAY FROM IT. IT CAME FROM NOWHERE; THE IDEA JUST CAME TO ME. IT'S DANGEROUS, ISN'T IT? YOU CAN MISS OUT ON A GOAL. BUT WHENEVER THE CHANCE COMES, I DO IT"

– BOBBY FIRMINO

NO-LOOK BOBBY

21

He's delivered goals and moments that have helped to bring trophies and success to Anfield – but as much as anything, Bobby Firmino has delivered entertainment. His skills have Kopites gasping in awe at times and his celebrations are something else, whether they come after his team-mates' goals or his own. One of his most popular tricks is the no-look pass or shot. Blink and you'll miss it, but Bobby avoids run-of-the-mill tap-ins where he can. While the traditional coaching manual might say 'keep your eye on the ball', the flamboyant Brazilian lines up his shot, but just before the moment of contact he swivels his head the other way and puts the ball in the net without looking. Risky. Cheeky. But very entertaining. These goals against Sevilla (2017) and West Ham (2018) are just two examples of his no-look finishes!

*WE'VE CONQUERED ALL OF EUROPE.
WE'RE NEVER GONNA STOP.*

*FROM PARIS DOWN TO TURKEY.
WE'VE WON THE F***ING LOT.*

*BOB PAISLEY AND BILL SHANKLY.
THE FIELDS OF ANFIELD ROAD.*

*WE ARE LOYAL SUPPORTERS
AND WE COME FROM LIVERPOOL…*

It was the scarf-twirling, eardrum-splitting, blood-pumping Kop chant that provided the backdrop to Liverpool's incredible run to the 2018 Champions League final in Kyiv and it is still sung just as passionately now. Based on a 1985 europop hit called L'Estate Sta Finendo [summer is ending] by Righeira, Allez Allez Allez was first adopted by supporters of southern Italian club L'Aquila Calcio in 2009 before followers of Napoli and later Porto later devised their own versions. Kopite Phil Howard saw a YouTube video of Porto fans singing it in Dortmund in 2016, his mate Liam Malone wrote the lyrics to the Liverpool version in 2017 and after initially being sung on away coaches it finally caught on in February 2018 when – ironically – Liverpool

I FEEL FINE

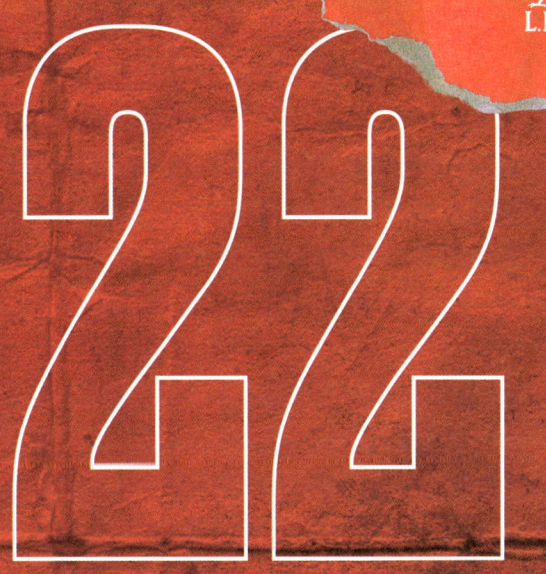

beat Porto 5-0 in Estadio do Dragao. Jamie Webster was among the travelling Kop that night, added it to his repertoire when playing in the Halfway House pub after a 2-0 Anfield win against Newcastle in early March and a YouTube video from that night went viral. When the Reds faced Manchester City in the Champions League quarter-final in April 2018, Anfield rocked to the sound of Allez Allez Allez and ahead of the the Champions League final in Kyiv, Webster released a version on iTunes that made over £8,000 for local charity An Hour For Others. Allez Allez Allez is now instantly recognisable as an Anfield anthem and when it comes to singing it to back the Redmen, we're never gonna stop.

23 ROMA RATTLED

Riding high on the crest of a wave after beating Porto and Manchester City 5-0 and 5-1 on aggregate in the knock-out stages of the 2017/18 Champions League, Liverpool were bubbling with confidence when AS Roma arrived on Merseyside for the semi-final first leg. The Italians had Alisson Becker in goal, but as Anfield crackled to the sound of Allez Allez Allez, even he couldn't stop the rampant Reds. Liverpool's front three tore into I Giallorossi with Mo Salah at his exceptional best. He curled home the opener off the underside of the crossbar, lifted the ball over Alisson to make it 2-0, crossed for Sadio Mane to add a third and teed up Roberto Firmino for Liverpool's fourth. When our number nine headed home James Milner's corner in the 69th minute, the Reds had become only the second side to score five goals in a Champions League semi-final. The visitors got a couple of late goals back, but the Romans had been well and truly rattled by one of the finest displays of attacking football Anfield had ever witnessed on the European stage.

SEÁN COX

24

Liverpool's 5-2 win against AS Roma will also sadly be remembered for an awful pre-match incident. Lifelong supporter Seán Cox, who had travelled from Dunboyne, Republic of Ireland, to watch his beloved Reds, was left in a coma after being attacked outside the ground by Roma hooligans. Tragically, Seán suffered permanent brain damage and it was two years before he was able to return to his family home in County Meath. The players held aloft a banner in support of Seán after the semi-final second leg in Roma's Stadio Olimpico and Jürgen Klopp was upset by what had happened. "I would trade any of the glory that could come our way for Seán to get back to full health and to be back at home with you and all of his loved ones," he wrote in a letter to Seán's wife, Martina. Seven months later, Seán was able to return to Anfield for the first time and after seeing Liverpool beat Manchester City 3-1 in the Premier League, he met the Reds boss. "Seeing Seán at Anfield was definitely one of the high points for all of us," said Klopp. In April 2022, Seán made his first post-pandemic return to Anfield for the Champions League semi-final against Villarreal and met Sir Kenny Dalglish, Ian Rush and Virgil van Dijk among others, but it was something that Klopp said to Seán's family that is the measure of the man. "Whatever you need, and when no authority in this country or your country can help, I think we can always find a way where we can make things maybe easier. We still feel this. It's like friendship, it's like family, it's like we really have to do these things because we want to do these things. That's the moment when the club has to show real unity, because it's not about who's responsible for it, it's about who helps after what happened."

OX'S ORIGAMI

When Alex Oxlade-Chamberlain went down with a knee injury during Liverpool's 5-2 Champions League semi-final win against AS Roma at Anfield in April 2018, nobody knew the true horror of the damage. For three months, so as not to distract from the Reds' attempts to win the Champions League, the Liverpool midfielder kept the news to himself. When it then transpired that Ox had damaged every ligament in his right knee – the cruciate, medial and lateral collateral ligaments plus a tendon leading to his hamstring – and wouldn't play again for 12 months there was shock among LFC supporters. In Asia, members of the Japanese Official Liverpool Supporters Club felt compelled to send Oxlade-Chamberlain a special 'get well soon' message. They asked Liverpool supporters in Japan to write words of support, fold them into paper cranes and send them in. Traditionally in Japan, 'one thousand paper cranes' are made while praying for someone to recover from illness or injury and that's precisely what the Japanese OLSC made for the Ox. It took 10 Japan OLSC members 90 days to piece together, using strings and needles, and in November 2018 Tokyo-based member Yujiro Sagawa travelled to Melwood to present the gift to Alex. "To know that people in Japan have taken that much time to put together something like this for me is amazing," said Oxlade-Chamberlain. "Things like this blow my mind. I can't thank fans of the Japan supporters' club enough for this wonderful gift." It was a colourful reminder that no matter where Liverpool fans are in the world, the support for our players is second to none.

Standard
Chartered

Standard
Chartered

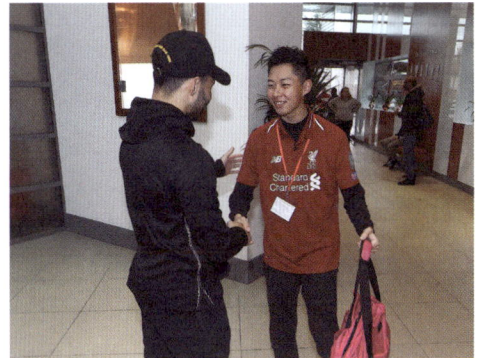

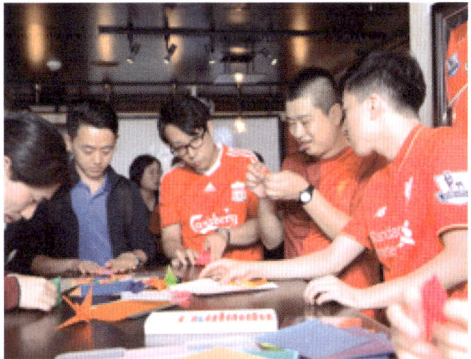

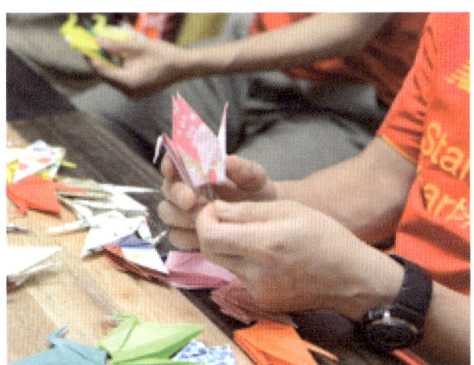

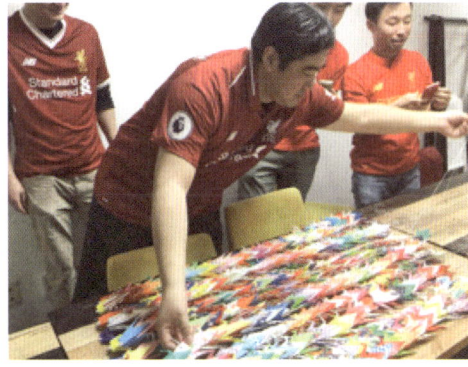

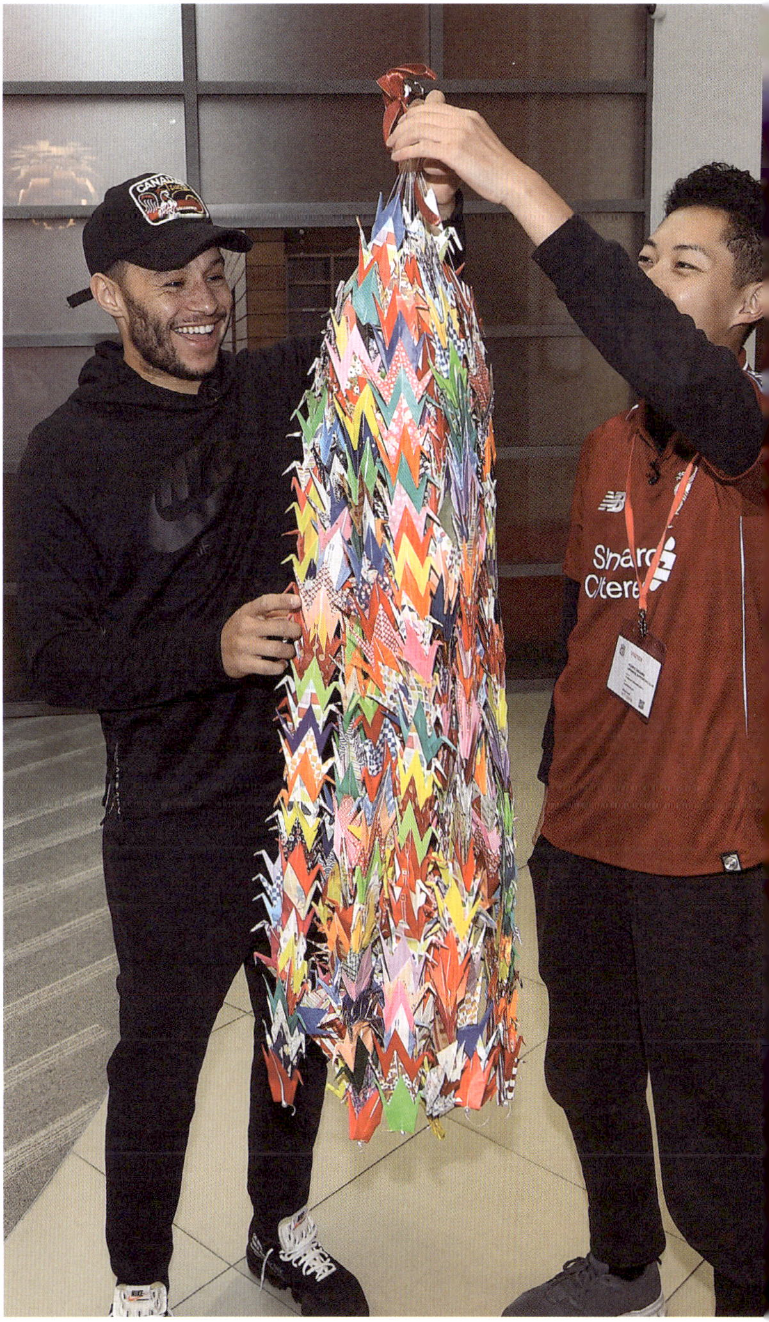

I FEEL FINE

Most goals in a 38-game Premier League season

32	Mo Salah	Liverpool	2017/18
31	Luis Suarez	Liverpool	2013/14
31	Cristiano Ronaldo	Manchester Utd	2007/08
31	Alan Shearer	Blackburn Rovers	1995/96
30	Harry Kane	Tottenham	2017/18
30	Robin van Persie	Arsenal	2011/12
30	Thierry Henry	Arsenal	2003/04
30	Kevin Phillips	Sunderland	1999/2000

I FEEL FINE

26

ONE-SEASON WONDER?

It's easy to forget following season after season of consistent Mo Salah goals that there were many who doubted his ability to find the back of the net when he arrived from Roma in the summer of 2017. As it turned out, that first season was a blockbuster one for the prolific Egyptian as he hit 44 in all competitions – and he's hardly stopped scoring since. He netted in the first game of the season, at Watford, and kept adding to his total. By the time the final Premier League match arrived against Brighton at Anfield, Salah needed just one more to set the record for the most goals in a 38-game Premier League season – and he took just 26 minutes to do so, receiving Dominic Solanke's pass and slotting past Matt Ryan. The Reds went on to win 4-0 with Solanke and Andy Robertson grabbing their first Liverpool goals, but it was Salah's 32nd league strike that grabbed the headlines – and he picked up many trophies, including his Premier League Golden Boot, after the match. It wouldn't be the last time he collected one of those.

BOSS

They've become known for the huge pre-match gatherings of travelling Kopites before Champions League finals in Kyiv's Shevchenko Park, Madrid's Plaza Felipe II and Cours de Vincennes in Paris, but BOSS Nights began as a spin-off from a Liverpool fanzine. A BOSS Mag was launched in 2007 by Dan Nicholson and friends – Reds who would go to Anfield in the afternoon followed by a gig in the evening. With many of the lads being in bands they hit upon the idea of putting on their own gigs and in August 2011, after Liverpool played Sunderland, the first show was held at the Static Gallery on Berry Street. Not a single LFC chant was sung. In May 2013, a teenager called Jamie Webster played on stage for the first time and in 2014, as Liverpool challenged for the Premier League title, chants broke out in the BOSS Night crowd at Sound on Duke Street. Webster strummed along to 'Here's to You, Jordan Henderson,' video footage of it spread on social media and from there a new, unique fan culture of Liverpool supporters attending a post-match gig where musicians played Anfield songs and chants organically emerged. In 2018, with the support of LFC, the first BOSS Night abroad was held before the Champions League final in Ukraine and since then it has been taken on tour all over the world from Qatar to America and Germany to Thailand. The sea of Reds at the Madrid 2019 and Paris 2022 BOSS Nights ahead of the Champions League finals provided some truly astonishing scenes, and while the heartbeat of this incredible cultural phenomenon that has featured bands such as Cast and the Lightning Seeds will always be in Liverpool, it has unquestionably brought Reds from all over the world together to share and celebrate a passion that binds us all.

I FEEL FINE

I FEEL FINE

GOODBYE PEP, HELLO PEP

"Pep is unique. I've never met anyone like him before and I'm not sure I'll be fortunate enough to do so again in the future. He is studious and coaching-obsessed; he believes in the training process with a passion I've never seen before." These are the words of Jürgen Klopp when describing one of his most important right-hand men, Pep Lijnders. He was commenting on the Dutchman in the foreword to his book 'Intensity', which is the perfect illustration of Lijnders' dedication to coaching and the evolution of the Liverpool team. In the book Pep describes the ideas behind the club's training methods, the preparation for every match, and how everything knits together with the manager's philosophy to produce a successful machine on the pitch. Lijnders was already a Liverpool coach when Jürgen Klopp arrived in 2015, but he left in 2018 to become NEC Nijmegen manager. He was back at Anfield that summer and has been Klopp's trusted assistant through all the recent successes, even taking the reins when the boss was struck down by COVID-19 during the 2021/22 season. When Klopp signed a new contract with Liverpool in 2022, Lijnders and other members of his staff including Peter Krawietz and Vitor Matos extended their deals too. This winning combination has lots more still to achieve.

DIVOCK LOVES A DERBY

It's a horrible way to lose a derby match, but it's an absolutely brilliant way to win one. And there's no doubt that Divock Origi knows how to make a late impact. The mercurial forward was summoned from the bench with six minutes remaining of a tight contest in December 2018 that the Reds were desperate to win to stay in touch with Manchester City at the top of the table. But with the clock ticking well into added time, the breakthrough looked like it would never come. Trent Alexander-Arnold pumped one final deep cross towards the area which Yerry Mina headed to Virgil van Dijk. The Dutchman's swipe goalwards spun into the air and looked like it would either loop into the goalkeeper's arms or drop onto the top of the net. It did neither. An uncertain Jordan Pickford tried to grasp the ball but it spilled in front of goal where Origi was ready to pounce and nodded it into the empty net. The fact that the game had looked like finishing goalless only made the moment sweeter. Jürgen Klopp raced onto the pitch to embrace Alisson, Anfield went crazy and Origi had another chapter of his Liverpool legacy written. Origi finished his LFC career with six derby goals, making Everton the team he scored most Liverpool goals against.

I FEEL FINE

Divock's derby goals

20 April 2016	Premier League	4-0
1 April 2017	Premier League	3-1
2 December 2018	**Premier League**	**1-0**
4 December 2019	Premier League	5-2 (2)
24 April 2022	Premier League	2-0

ADDED-TIME WINNER

29

I FEEL FINE

NEVER GIVE UP

At best it seemed optimistic; at worst a little delusional. But when Mo Salah was spotted walking around the Anfield pitch in a black t-shirt displaying white lettering that read 'Never Give Up' he probably had no idea how iconic that garment would turn out to be. The occasion was the second leg of the 2019 Champions League semi-final against Barcelona. The metaphor 'The Reds had a mountain to climb' is no exaggeration. Despite playing well in the first leg at Camp Nou, Jürgen Klopp's men came away with a 3-0 defeat. No away goals and facing the might of a Barça team that contained the likes of Luis Suarez, Gerard Pique, Sergio Busquets and the incomparable Lionel Messi seemed like an impossible task. Then add in the fact that a Liverpool team that needed four goals to win the tie would be without two of their feared front line in Bobby Firmino and Salah, and it reduced the chances of success from small to wafer-thin. Well, we all know what happened next. Salah would be seen again a few hours later celebrating with his team-mates in that 'Never Give Up' t-shirt in front of the Kop after one of the most memorable matches ever staged at Anfield.

"THERE'S HOPE AND IT'S FOOTBALL. WE ARE NOT IN A SITUATION WHERE WE SAY IT WILL HAPPEN 100% BUT IT'S FOOTBALL. THE CHARACTER OF THE BOYS....TWO OF THE WORLD'S BEST STRIKERS ARE NOT AVAILABLE AND WE HAVE TO SCORE FOUR GOALS TO GO THROUGH IN 90 MINUTES. AS LONG AS WE HAVE 11 PLAYERS ON THE PITCH WE WILL TRY FOR 90 MINUTES TO CELEBRATE THE CHAMPIONS LEAGUE CAMPAIGN TO GIVE IT A PROPER FINISH. THAT'S THE PLAN. IF WE CAN DO IT, WONDERFUL. IF WE CAN'T DO IT, LET'S FAIL IN THE MOST BEAUTIFUL WAY"

– JÜRGEN KLOPP (PRE-MATCH)

"IT MEANS SO MUCH TO ALL OF US. THERE ARE MORE IMPORTANT THINGS IN THE WORLD, BUT CREATING THIS EMOTIONAL ATMOSPHERE TOGETHER IS SO SPECIAL. IT'S ALL ABOUT THE PLAYERS. THE MIX OF POTENTIAL AND UNBELIEVABLE HEART IS JUST A MIX I NEVER SAW BEFORE. IT SHOWS WHAT'S POSSIBLE IN FOOTBALL. IT'S SO NICE"

– JÜRGEN KLOPP (POST-MATCH)

I FEEL FINE

31
"CORNER TAKEN QUICKLY..."

It's the most famous corner in Liverpool's long history. Not only was it a quick-thinking piece of genius, it also came at a crucial time in a massive game and completed one of the greatest comebacks Reds fans had ever witnessed en route to collecting European Cup number six in 2019. Jürgen Klopp's men had remarkably overturned a 3-0 first-leg deficit to be level with Barcelona at Anfield in the Champions League semi-final second leg with around 12 minutes to go thanks to a goal from Divock Origi and a double from substitute Gini Wijnaldum. A corner was won at the Kop end. As Trent Alexander-Arnold received a ball from Academy forward turned ballboy Oakley Cannonier, Origi rolled a spare ball off the pitch then trotted to the centre of the box, around eight yards out. As the Catalans' defence tried to draw breath, the Reds' right-back spotted Origi unmarked, delivered a precise low cross. And the rest is history – immortalised further by LFCTV commentator Steve Hunter's ecstatic commentary...

"TWELVE MINUTES TO GO IN NORMAL TIME... LIVERPOOL 3-0...CORNER TAKEN QUICKLY, ORIGI!... THEY'VE DONE IT!... UNBELIEVABLE!... DIVOCK ORIGI!... OH, MY WORD!..."

I FEEL FINE

THIS WAS BARCELONA'S HEAVIEST-EVER DEFEAT AGAINST AN ENGLISH SIDE IN ALL EUROPEAN COMPETITIONS

UEFA Champions League semi-final second leg

Liverpool 4   Barcelona 0
Origi (7, 79),
Wijnaldum (54, 56)
(Liverpool win 4-3 on aggregate)

Liverpool: Alisson, Alexander-Arnold, Van Dijk, Matip, Robertson (Wijnaldum 46), Fabinho, Milner, Henderson, Shaqiri (Sturridge 90), Origi (Gomez 85), Mane

Barcelona: Ter Stegen, Roberto, Pique, Lenglet, Alba, Rakitic (Malcom 80), Busquets, Vidal (Melo 75), Coutinho (Semedo 60), Suarez, Messi

GOALS FROM SUBS

The iconic Barcelona semi-final in 2019 is one of the best examples of substitutes having a goalscoring impact on a game for the Reds. Gini Wijnaldum replaced Andy Robertson at half-time and nine minutes later he found the net, and equalised with a brilliant header two minutes after that. One of Liverpool's greatest goalscoring subs, Divock Origi, finished off the job that night – though he was on the pitch from the start on this occasion. Wijnaldum admitted afterwards that his performance may have been motivated, in part, by the fact he was disappointed at being left on the bench in the first place. "I'm really emotional because I was really angry at the manager that he put me on the bench!" he admitted. "I had to do something when I came on, I had to help the team...but overall it was a team performance." Up to the end of the 2021/22 season, Origi is the joint-highest goalscorer from the bench during Jürgen Klopp's time at the club with 12 – the most valuable probably coming in the 2019 Champions League final, setting the seal on the 2-0 win against Tottenham. Bobby Firmino also has 12 goals from substitute appearances since October 2015, while Christian Benteke scored the first goal from the bench of the Klopp era in a 1-1 draw with Southampton in the manager's third game in charge.

I FEEL FINE

I FEEL FINE

I FEEL FINE

Goals from subs in the Klopp era (as of 01/09/22)

Divock Origi 12
Roberto Firmino 12
Daniel Sturridge 8
Mo Salah 6
Christian Benteke 6
Diogo Jota 5
Alex Oxlade-Chamberlain 3
Xherdan Shaqiri 3
James Milner 3
Takumi Minamino 3
Gini Wijnaldum 3
Sadio Mane 2
Jordon Ibe 2
Adam Lallana 2
Fabinho 2
Darwin Nunez 2
Fabio Carvalho 2
Sheyi Ojo 1
Ben Woodburn 1
Philippe Coutinho 1
Jordan Henderson 1
Joel Matip 1
Curtis Jones 1
Naby Keita 1
Harvey Elliott 1
Luis Diaz 1

33

EXTENDED WARM WELCOME

The atmosphere inside Anfield is legendary – especially for the biggest league games and huge European occasions. Many players have spoken about it and Jürgen Klopp is certainly a manager who likes to harness fan power to give his team a boost. So why not spread the Anfield atmosphere outside the stadium so the players can feel the passion before they've even arrived at the ground? That's what Liverpool supporters have become more and more accustomed to doing in recent seasons. Matches during title run-ins have seen fans lining the streets, particularly along Anfield Road, in colourful fashion, singing, clapping and waving as the bus drives past. European nights – especially in the crucial knock-out rounds – have seen supporters particularly vocal, and first-team players have been known to record the welcome on their phones, such has been the impact of fan fervour. It might only add one per cent to the Reds' overall performance – but it's one per cent Liverpool fanatics are happy to give.

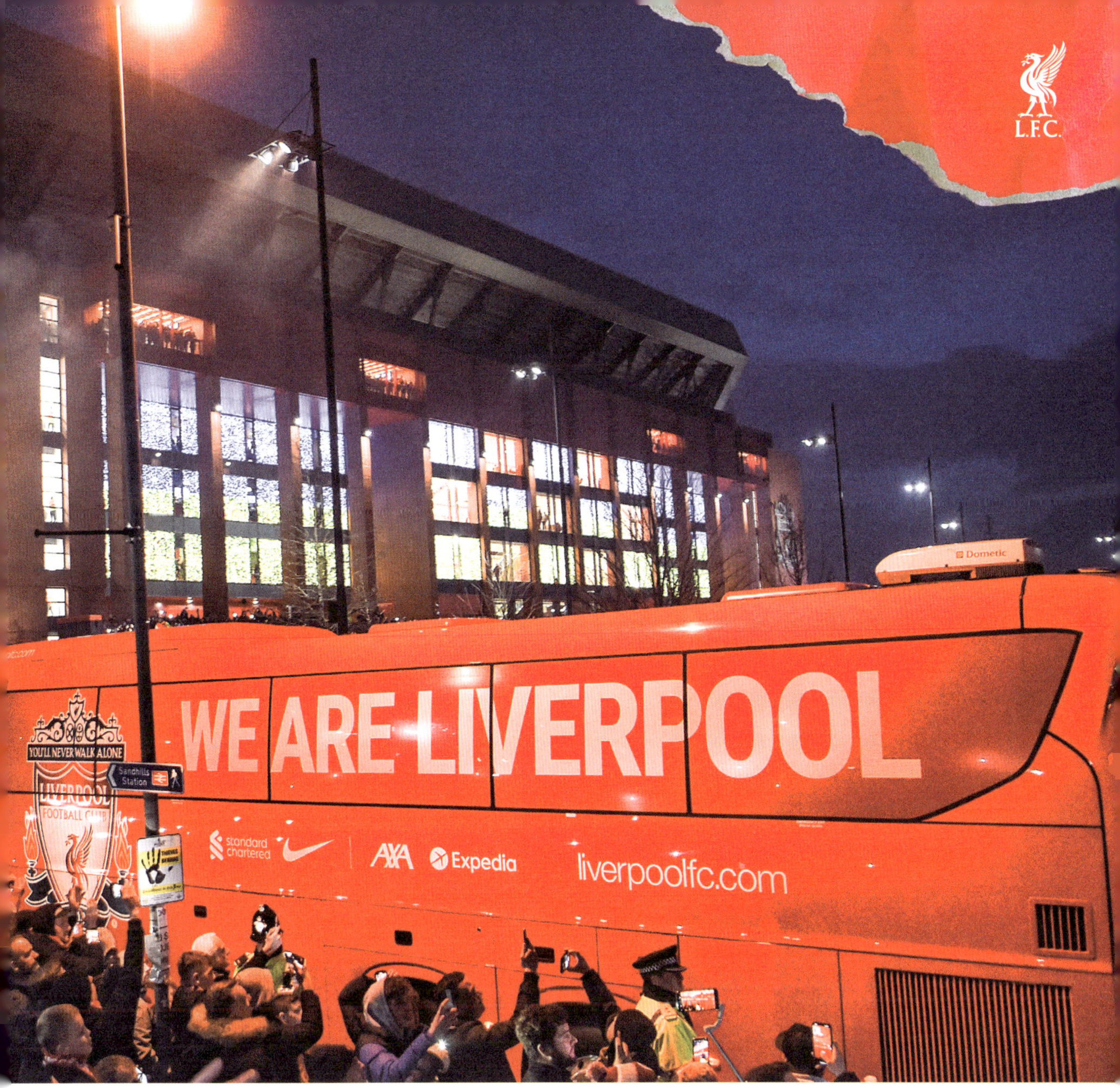
L.F.C.
WE ARE LIVERPOOL
YOU'LL NEVER WALK ALONE
LIVERPOOL FOOTBALL CLUB
Sandhills Station
standard chartered
AXA
Expedia
liverpoolfc.com
Dometic

TSIMIKAS
21

YOU'LL NEVER WALK ALONE

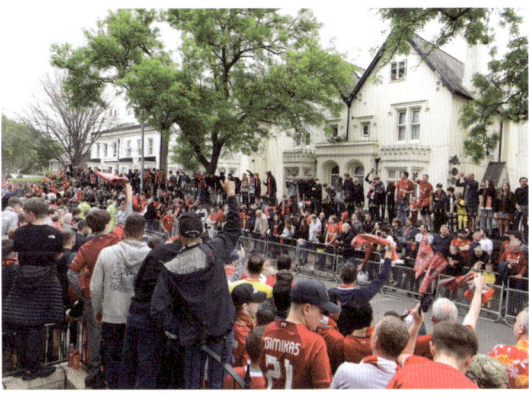

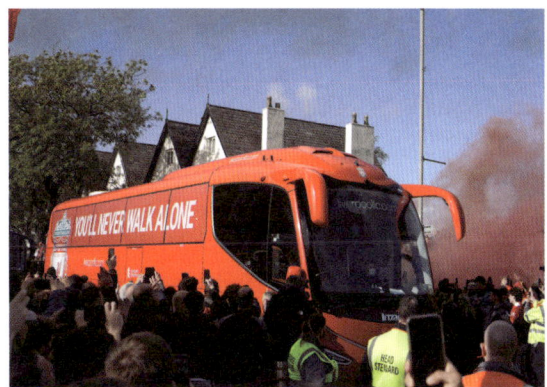

I FEEL FINE

ALISSON WONDERLAND

Liverpool Football Club has been blessed to have some of the best goalkeepers around, and in Alisson Becker it was obvious pretty early on that he could be a difference-maker for the Reds. The first time many Liverpool supporters will have set eyes on the big Brazilian was when he was conceding five goals in the Champions League semi-final first leg for Roma at Anfield – so it will have raised a few eyebrows when a large fee was spent on bringing him to the club. Those eyebrows were very soon relaxed again after seeing him winning the Premier League Golden Glove award in his first season in a Liverpool shirt. Calm in possession, technically excellent and an intimidating force in one-on-one situations, Alisson's first 12 months at the club were a triumph. He was instrumental in the club reaching their highest points total (at that point) in a Premier League season, accumulating 97 when finishing just behind Manchester City. That total was partly down to the 21 clean sheets Alisson and the team amassed. His presence was crucial in the run to becoming champions of Europe that season too. He kept Barcelona scoreless in the semi-final second leg, made sure Tottenham drew a blank in the final – and without his amazing save in the final group game from Napoli's Arkadiusz Milik, the Reds wouldn't have made the knock-out stages at all. He claimed the Premier League Golden Glove trophy in that first season, an award he may have claimed again the following year, had injury not intervened, but he shared it with City's Ederson in 2021/22. He also collected the Champions League Golden Glove and Copa America equivalent in 2019. Even without the awards, there isn't a keeper in world football Liverpool fans would swap him for.

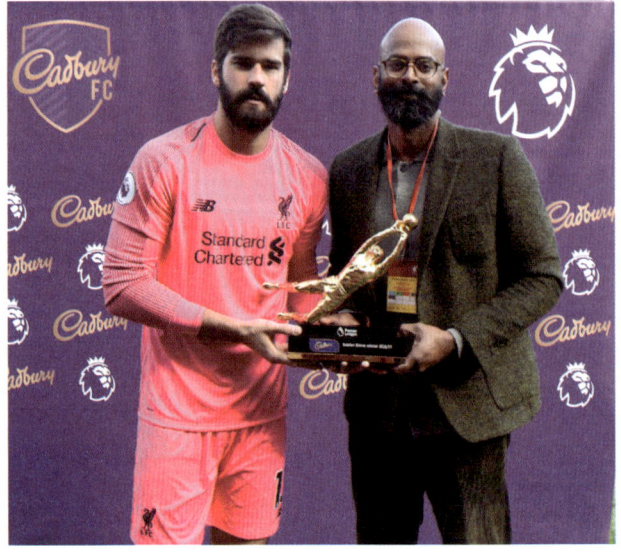

I FEEL FINE

I FEEL FINE

35

THE HENDO SHUFFLE

It's a sight that has become gloriously familiar in recent seasons and it all began with the Champions League final victory in Madrid in 2019. Mo Salah's early penalty set the Reds on the road to victory and Divock Origi's precise finish made certain of glory. The final whistle went, celebrations began and then the moment of truth as the players collected their medals and the skipper – as tradition dictates – stepped forward to lift Ol' Big Ears. Tradition, however, didn't dictate the manner in which Jordan Henderson raised Europe's finest trophy. He gave the cup a kiss, carried it over to his team-mates and with his back to the rest of the world he repeatedly stamped his feet on the floor before turning to raise the trophy to the sky. "I didn't really plan on doing that, to be honest," said Henderson. "It was a little bit of banter in the changing rooms prior. Robbo was messing about, he'd always do the shuffle pretending to lift the trophy. So, when the time came I felt as though I just wanted to sort of do it together and use that sort of banter that we'd had previously in terms of the little shuffle and stuff. I just wanted to be able to see the lads' faces just before I lifted it as well. That was really special for me, to be able to see the lads rather than just have my back to them. So, yeah, it was a little bit off the cuff, to be honest. After we did that [for] the Champions League the lads made sure I kept on doing it for the Super Cup and Club World Cup." And he's been true to his word, doing the 'Hendo shuffle' at every trophy-lift since.

TEARS OF JOY

You would have to have a heart of stone not to be moved by the warm, tearful embrace Jordan Henderson shared with his father in the aftermath of the 2019 Champions League final. The first major trophy Henderson had claimed as Reds' skipper brought an outpouring of emotion from the Liverpool midfielder. As the players walked around the perimeter of the pitch, Hendo spotted his father among the jubilant faces in the crowd. They met at pitchside and embraced for what seemed like an eternity. Proud dad Brian Henderson, who had successfully battled against cancer in the preceding years, had predicted that Jordan would play in a Champions League final one day. This was Henderson's second final, of course, but winning brought a much more powerful response than simply playing in the showpiece occasion. Brian has since seen his son lift many more trophies as LFC captain, but it's hard to imagine there would ever be a more emotional moment than they shared in Madrid.

LIFT-OFF FOR THE BOSS

37

A season of hard work where the Reds had come within a whisker of winning the Premier League got the outcome it deserved in the final match in Madrid. The squad had a togetherness and spirit that had seen it lose only once in the league all season and the relief at finally getting tangible reward was palpable. When the final whistle went at the end of the 2019 Champions League final there was laughter, joy, tears and love – especially for the manager who had brought everything together. The players hoisted him up and threw him into the air several times – safely catching him on each occasion!

"THIS MAY BE THE BEST NIGHT OF MY LIFE, PROFESSIONAL WISE. THIS IS SO IMPORTANT. TONIGHT IT'S REALLY EMOTIONAL. I AM OVERWHELMED TO BE HONEST BUT I'M MUCH CALMER THAN I THOUGHT I WOULD BE WHEN IT FINALLY HAPPENED. I FEEL MOSTLY RELIEVED. RELIEVED FOR MY FAMILY BECAUSE THE LAST SIX TIMES WE WERE AWAY ON HOLIDAY AND ALWAYS WITH A SILVER MEDAL AND THAT DOESN'T FEEL SO COOL. THIS IS FOR THE BOYS, THE FANS AND FOR THE OWNERS. FOR THE PLAYERS, THEY WERE PRETTY MUCH CRYING ON THE PITCH BECAUSE IT WAS SO EMOTIONAL, SO BIG, AND IT MEANS SO MUCH TO US. I HAVE SAT HERE MANY TIMES EXPLAINING HOW WE LOST THIS GAME. NOW I DON'T WANT TO EXPLAIN WHY WE WON I JUST WANT TO ENJOY THAT WE WON"

– JÜRGEN KLOPP

I FEEL FINE

38
LET'S TALK ABOUT SIX

Post-match celebrations after the Madrid final went well beyond what happened on the pitch at the Metropolitano Stadium. Back in Liverpool there were hundreds of thousands of people who wanted to join in the fun and show how proud they were of the team and the manager. And possibly the most iconic moment of a memorable bus parade around the streets of the city involved Jürgen Klopp. The Reds boss was sitting at the back of the top deck of the bus with a leg hanging over the side and a black baseball cap on. With a concentrated expression on his face, he looked down at his hands and began counting his fingers. Putting one digit up at a time he got to five, paused momentarily, and then put up a thumb on his other hand to make it six, adding a cheeky smile as he joked with the supporters below. A GIF was born and the message was clear: let's talk about six, baby.

I FEEL FINE

TURNING THE CITY RED

Liverpool knows how to celebrate. There is no better city in the world for putting on a party – and in recent years the red section of the community has had a team that has given it a few excuses for getting out on the streets to mark their achievements. In Jürgen Klopp's time as Liverpool manager, the 2019 European Cup triumph brought hundreds of thousands onto the streets – and by the time the bus containing the players arrived on The Strand after a multi-mile trophy parade...WOW (to use a word popular with the boss). The Premier League title happened during the darker days of the COVID-19 pandemic, so by 2022, with the FA Cup and League Cup recently pocketed, the city was ready to rock again – despite the fact the Reds had lost out in the Champions League final the night before. Klopp was gobsmacked by the reception his team received in the wake of such an agonising defeat. "Without a shadow of a doubt, no club in the world – this world – that they lost the Champions League final the night before and the people arrive here in the shape they are, the mood they are. Absolutely outstanding. This is the best club in the world – I don't care what other people think!"

"IT'S AMAZING, YOU HAVE TO REALLY EXPERIENCE IT. I THINK THERE'S STILL MORE TO COME BUT IT'S ALREADY BEEN PAST MY EXPECTATIONS"
– VIRGIL VAN DIJK IN 2019

"THAT'S THE BEST SIGN YOU CAN GET: YOU DON'T HAVE TO WIN, YOU JUST NEED TO PUT ALL THAT YOU HAVE IN, REALLY THROW EVERYTHING ON THE PITCH AND THE PEOPLE OF LIVERPOOL LOVE YOU"

– JÜRGEN KLOPP

I FEEL FINE

"IT'S FOR THE PEOPLE, THAT WE CELEBRATE THAT WE ARE TOGETHER IN THIS MOMENT. THAT'S ALREADY ENOUGH TO ORGANISE A PARADE WITHOUT ANY TROPHIES"
– JÜRGEN KLOPP

I FEEL FINE

THIS IS WHO WE ARE...

'WE WIN CUPS'. Three simple words – but when displayed in huge white type on a plain red background, the words become so powerful. The flags and banners Kopites lovingly create and enthusiastically display to fellow supporters and the world at large are part of what make our club great. The creativity, humour and dedication put into them has gone on for years and with every passing season – sometimes every passing week – new flags and banners emerge. Every home game has fans scanning the Kop, in particular, to see if a new flag has been added. European finals see fans dominate city squares, parks and plazas with their red and

white banners draped on railings and hanging from windows. Wembley finals usually show the huge difference in approach between rival clubs as Liverpool supporters bring their homemade flags and banners with them, while opponents usually make less effort. During the COVID pandemic, Anfield was still covered in banners to provide the players with a reminder of the supporters who couldn't attend matches. Most of all, the flags and banners are a symbol of our identity. Like the songs we sing, they tell the world who we are, who we love and why we're so devoted to our club. We are Liverpool and these are our calling cards...

CLAPS FOR KEEPERS

Dating back to the days of Elisha Scott, Kopites have always had a special relationship with goalkeepers – particularly the ones who stand in front of the Kop goal. And there's a tradition that has carried on to this day. It goes without saying that whoever is trusted with the gloves for Liverpool always gets a rousing reception, but there can be few clubs where the away goalkeeper gets such an ovation from the supporters he hopes to disappoint for 90 minutes. Every visiting keeper is applauded as he makes his way to the Kop goal. Sometimes it takes them by surprise to receive such a welcome. Others ignore the hand of friendship and the applause turns to boos. Most enjoy the warm greeting, though the overall sentiment from the crowd is 'Welcome to Anfield; we hope you concede five!' In 2019, Adrian made his debut for Liverpool in dramatic circumstances. Late in the first half of the first game of the season against Norwich City, Alisson picked up an injury and the Spaniard had to quickly put on his gloves and jog towards the Kop goal. Any nerves must have been quickly quashed as he received a hero's welcome. The game finished 4-1 to the Reds and Adrian felt like part of the furniture already – which was good news with the UEFA Super Cup up for grabs days later...

I FEEL FINE

"I WANT TO THANK LIVERPOOL FANS FOR THE AFFECTION THEY SHOWED. THEY RESPECT PLAYERS A LOT. I'VE SPENT A LOT OF YEARS IN THIS COMPETITION AND COMING TO A STADIUM LIKE THIS AND BEING APPLAUDED LIKE THAT IS SUPERB"

– IKER CASILLAS, AFTER PLAYING FOR PORTO AT ANFIELD IN 2018

42

UEFA SUPER CUP

ADRIAAAA

It's usually been a tight affair whenever the Reds have met Chelsea in the last couple of decades. The same can be said of the UEFA Super Cup final between the teams in August 2019 – but while the match had to be decided on penalties, there was no little entertainment on show as both teams demonstrated how much they wanted to win this trophy. Indeed, in his post-match interviews, Jürgen Klopp likened the tussle to a boxing match, allowing him to do his best Rocky Balboa impression in saluting the unlikely hero...'Adriaaaannn'. Former West Ham keeper Adrian had joined the European champions that summer on a free transfer and was thrust into more action than he would have expected when Alisson was injured in the first Premier League match of the season. This was his first chance to help his new club win silverware and he was

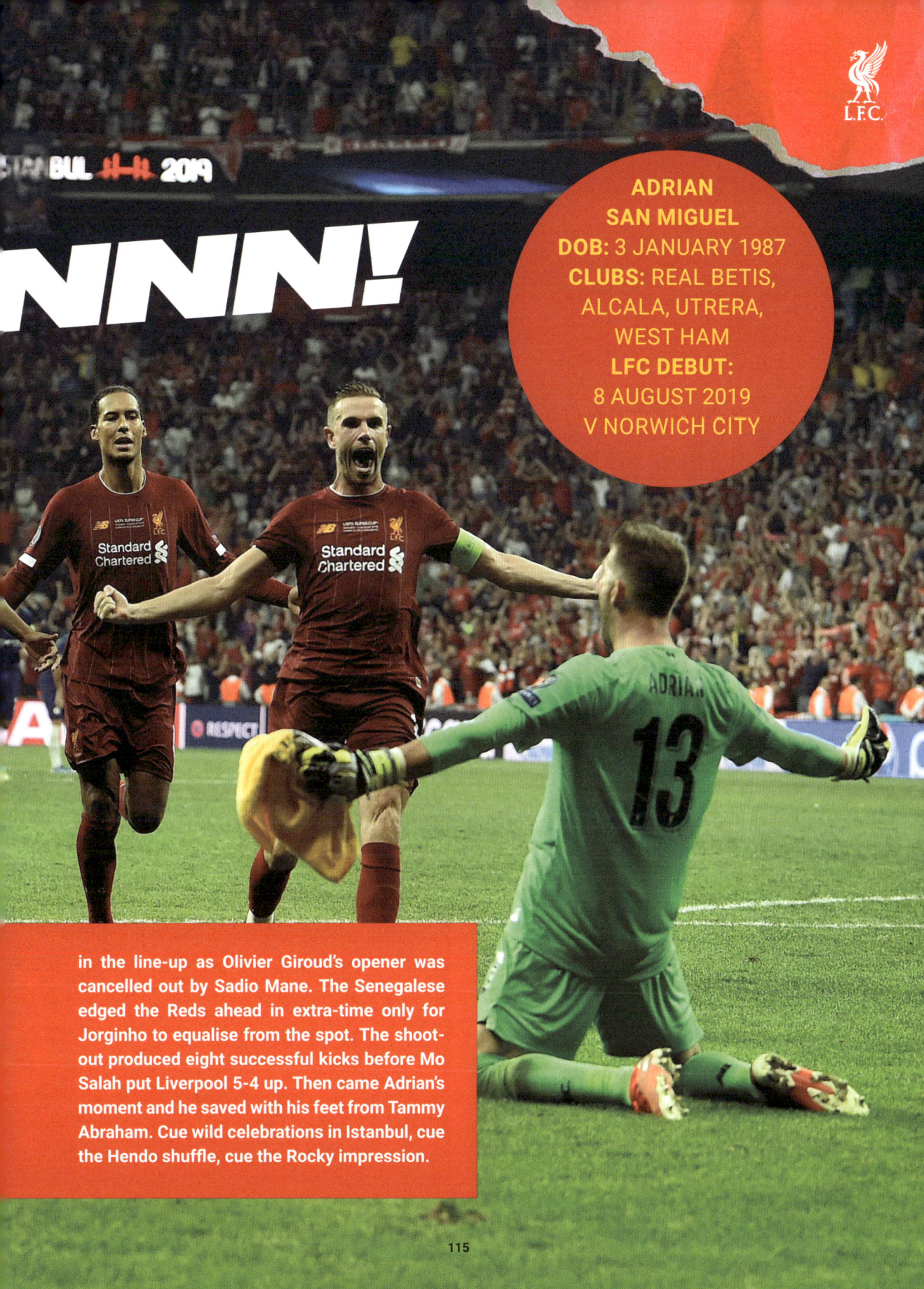

ADRIAN SAN MIGUEL
DOB: 3 JANUARY 1987
CLUBS: REAL BETIS, ALCALA, UTRERA, WEST HAM
LFC DEBUT: 8 AUGUST 2019 V NORWICH CITY

in the line-up as Olivier Giroud's opener was cancelled out by Sadio Mane. The Senegalese edged the Reds ahead in extra-time only for Jorginho to equalise from the spot. The shoot-out produced eight successful kicks before Mo Salah put Liverpool 5-4 up. Then came Adrian's moment and he saved with his feet from Tammy Abraham. Cue wild celebrations in Istanbul, cue the Hendo shuffle, cue the Rocky impression.

43
HIGH FIVES

"I don't know the last time when I had so much fun at a football game," beamed Jürgen Klopp after watching his side draw 5-5 with Arsenal at Anfield in the Carabao Cup before defeating the Gunners on penalties. "I really loved it! Maybe as a manager I should think more about or worry about the goals that we conceded, but I couldn't care less to be honest!" This 2019 fourth round tie was, incredibly, the first 5-5 draw that Liverpool had ever played out at Anfield, making it quite a night for Neco Williams to make his debut, for Harvey Elliott to become LFC's youngest starter – aged 16 years and 209 days old – and for Curtis Jones to net the winning penalty on his Anfield debut. Shkodran Mustafi's early own goal put the Reds in front, but then Arsenal led 3-1 and 4-2, James Milner scoring from a penalty. Long-range strikes from Alex Oxlade-Chamberlain and Divock Origi had the scoreboard showing 4-4 after 62 minutes and Arsenal thought they had won it through Joe Willock's 30-yarder until a stoppage-time Origi scissor-kick sent the match to spot-kicks. Caoimhin Kelleher saved from Dani Ceballos to leave Jones with the opportunity to send Liverpool through at the Kop end – a chance he didn't miss. "This is what you play football for," smiled the Scouse midfielder at full-time. It's fair to say his manager agreed.

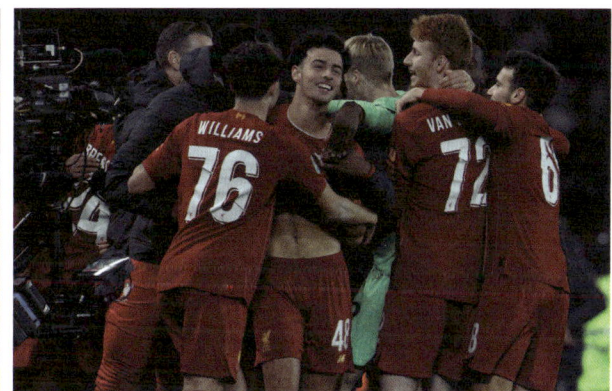

Carabao Cup fourth round, 30 October 2019

Liverpool 5
Mustafi (6 og)
Milner (43 pen)
Chamberlain (58)
Origi (62, 90+4)

Arsenal 5
Torreira (19)
Martinelli (26, 36)
Maitland-Niles (54)
Willock (70)

(Liverpool win 5-4 on pens – Milner, Lallana, Brewster, Origi, Jones)

44
THAT'S WHAT WE DO

A week before hosting Manchester City at Anfield in November 2019, and six points clear of the Cityzens at the top of the Premier League, unbeaten Liverpool trailed 1-0 at Aston Villa with 86 minutes on the clock. At precisely the same time, Kyle Walker was scoring an 86th-minute winner for City against Southampton at the Etihad. Had those results stayed the same, Pep Guardiola's men would arrive at Anfield knowing they could go top on goal difference with a victory, but then Jürgen Klopp's 'mentality monsters' (a phrase he had coined after a 3-1 win at Southampton in April 2019) turned up. Sadio Mane's cross was headed home by Andy Robertson at the far post and in the fourth minute of stoppage-time, Mane put his head in where it hurts to send a glancing header, from Trent Alexander-Arnold's corner, into the Villa net. It was absolute limbs in the away end. "That's what we do," quipped Virgil van Dijk to an LFCTV cameraman as he walked down the Villa Park tunnel. The following weekend at Anfield, Liverpool extended their Premier League advantage to nine points with a brilliant 3-1 victory against Manchester City, Fabinho, Mo Salah and Mane all on the scoresheet. It was only November, but it proved to be a crucial turning point in the 2019/20 Premier League title race.

I FEEL FINE

ADDED-TIME WINNER

THE REDS ARE TAKING OVER

"I would say, right now, it's the toughest stadium in Europe to go to," said Manchester City boss Pep Guardiola ahead of his team's visit to Anfield in November 2019. Liverpool headed into the encounter six points clear of the Cityzens, after winning 10 of their opening 11 games, and what followed felt like a seismic shift in the title race. While City were complaining they should have been awarded a penalty for handball, a Liverpool counter-attack was ending with Fabinho firing the ball past Claudio Bravo from 25 yards. The goal stood and seven minutes later the Anfield crowd was lapping up a goal reminiscent of Terry McDermott's seventh against Spurs in 1978. Trent Alexander-Arnold sprayed a glorious cross-field pass to Andy Robertson. He sent an angled cross towards Mo Salah, who planted a header into the net after letting the ball bounce once. When Sadio Mane's diving header put the Reds 3-0 up, City were done for, and although they got a late goal back, it was a decisive blow that had Kopites singing: "The Reds are taking over, Guardiola, Guardiola…"

I FEEL FINE

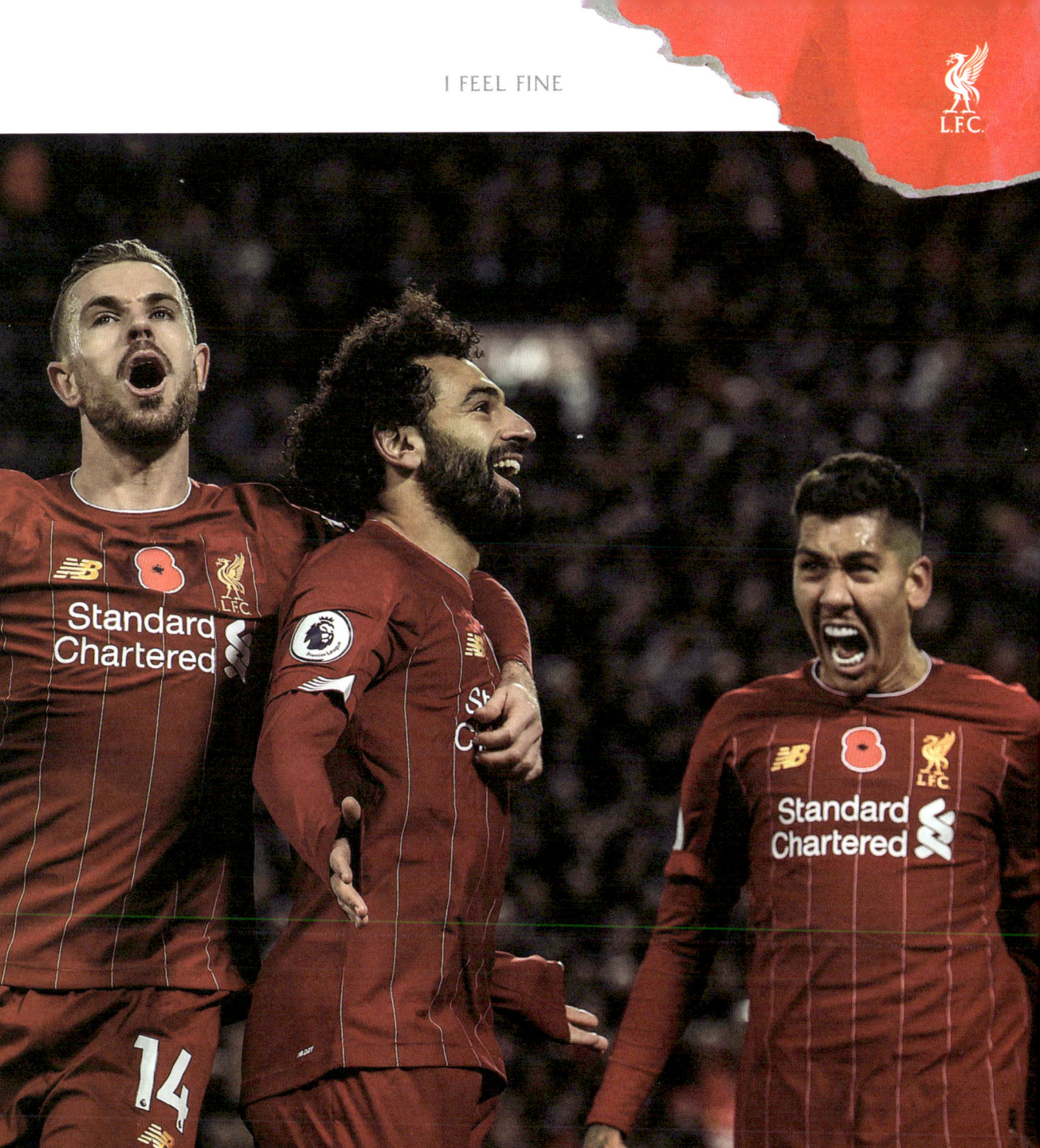

46 WE WON IT IN QATAR

'Monterrey, Flamengo, we're the greatest team by far, we're the mighty Liverpool, we won it in Qatar, we won it in Qatar...' Jürgen Klopp's European champions headed off to the gulf state in December 2019 intent on becoming the first Liverpool side to win the FIFA Club World Cup, but with Jordan Henderson playing at the back as Joe Gomez was the only fit centre-half, and Adam Lallana deputising for the injured Fabinho in the holding midfield role, the Redmen faced a tricky semi-final against Mexican side Monterrey. Naby Keita's early goal was cancelled out and it was only in the 91st minute, when Trent Alexander-Arnold crossed to fellow substitute Roberto Firmino, that the Reds booked a place in the final against Flamengo. A win for the Brazilians, who had beaten Liverpool 3-0 in Tokyo in the 1981 Intercontinental Cup, would complete a treble to make it their greatest ever season, but Virgil van Dijk returned from illness and it was to be Bobby's night. The final was in extra-time when he received a pull-back from Sadio Mane, delayed his shot to wrongfoot the goalkeeper and slotted home. Off came Firmino's shirt in celebration and when the final whistle blew the mighty Reds of Liverpool were club world champions for the first time, adding another prestigious honour to the list.

> "I SAID BEFORE THE GAME I DON'T KNOW EXACTLY HOW IT WOULD FEEL. NOW I CAN SAY IT'S OUTSTANDING, ABSOLUTELY SENSATIONAL. I'M SO PROUD OF THE BOYS AND IT COULDN'T BE BETTER"
>
> – JÜRGEN KLOPP

I FEEL FINE

"WE ARE REALLY HAPPY TO BE HERE AND WE ARE REALLY HAPPY THAT WE BRING THE TROPHY TO OUR CITY, TO OUR CLUB"

– ALISSON BECKER

I FEEL FINE

47
POWER PLAY

It had 'banana skin' written all over it. Not that a match away to Leicester City is ever a particularly easy fixture, but the high-flying Reds had only dropped two points in the league by the time they made the trip to the King Power Stadium for the Boxing Day fixture in 2019. The main problem for LFC was that the trip to Leicester was coming via Doha, Qatar. Having just made the exhausting and emotionally-draining journey to become FIFA club world champions, Jürgen Klopp's men had the perfect excuse for a below-par performance in Leicester. If anything, it had the opposite effect. Bobby Firmino nodded the Reds in front in the first half as the Redmen dominated. James Milner added the second from the penalty spot before Firmino beautifully finished off the third. The most memorable act of the night was saved until last as Trent Alexander-Arnold drilled a shot from the edge of the area that sealed a 4-0 win and allowed him the luxury of an arms-folded celebration in front of the ecstatic travelling Kop. Though nobody wanted to admit it just yet, the performance had the hallmark of champions.

I FEEL FINE

Leicester City 0
Liverpool 4

Firmino (31, 74)
Milner (71 pen)
Alexander-Arnold (78)

48

YOUNG BLOOD

Liverpool have always been a club that brings through young talents. Fowler, Owen, Gerrard and Carragher are just some of the Anfield stars of the past that began as starlets. That tradition has been very much kept alive during the Jürgen Klopp era with the best individual example being Trent Alexander-Arnold, who played in his third Champions League final at the tender age of 23, having made his debut as an 18-year-old. There was a great example of what young players can do when an inexperienced Liverpool team knocked Everton out of the FA Cup in January 2020. Curtis Jones, aged 18 at the time, scored the only goal of the tie to really show what confident young players are capable of. And in the following round the Reds fielded their youngest ever starting line-up, with an average age of just over 19. Five players made their debuts as the Reds beat Shrewsbury Town 1-0.

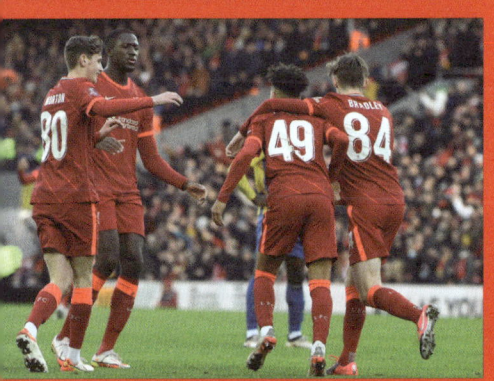

I FEEL FINE

LFC's youngest debutants under Jürgen Klopp

Harvey Elliott
16 years 5 months 21 days
25.09.2019 v MK Dons (LC)

James Norris
16 years 8 months 13 days
17.12.2019 v Aston Villa (LC)

Kaide Gordon
16 years 11 months 16 days
21.09.2021 v Norwich City (LC)

Ki-Jana Hoever
16 years 11 months 20 days
26.09.2012 v Wolves (FA Cup)

Ben Woodburn
17 years 1 month 11 days
26.11.2016 v Sunderland (PL)

49
ON THE SLIDE

It was probably the moment even the most cynical and weathered Liverpool supporter started to believe the 30-year wait for a league title win was soon to end. It was a goal that sealed a 2-0 win against fierce rivals Manchester United at Anfield to make it 21 wins from 22 Premier League games and put the Reds 16 points clear at the top of the table. It was only January, too. One goal up following Virgil van Dijk's first-half header, a series of chances to seal victory had come and gone as the match ticked into added time. Alisson collected the ball after a tame United effort and spotted Mo Salah in space near the halfway line. A pinpoint kick set Salah through on goal and the Egyptian King sped clear and did the rest. The Kop went wild, Salah threw his shirt off, and who was the first man to greet him as he turned around? Alisson raced past all his other team-mates and produced a 10-metre knee-slide to get there first. Almost every Kopite inside the stadium bellowed 'And now yer gonna believe us, we're gonna win the league' with more passion and certainty than at any point since last winning the title in 1990.

I FEEL FINE

Premier League table (top 6, 19.1.2020)

	P	W	Pts
Liverpool	22	21	64
Man City	23	15	48
Leicester City	23	14	45
Chelsea	23	12	39
Man United	23	9	34
Wolves	23	8	34

50

BOB AND EMLYN

Standing at 8ft tall and at an appropriate height for selfies and photos, the bronze statue of Bob Paisley carrying Emlyn Hughes was unveiled at Anfield's Paisley Square on 30 January 2020. Commissioned by club sponsors Standard Chartered, as part of a year-long celebration of Paisley's life and legacy 100 years after he was born, the statue is based upon a photo taken during a Liverpool v Tottenham Hotspur match in April 1968. When 20-year-old Hughes suffered a gashed knee in the first minute of the second half, 49-year-old Paisley – Liverpool's trainer at the time – lifted 'Crazy Horse' onto his shoulders and carried him off for treatment. Created by sculptor Andy Edwards, the statue epitomises what Paisley, who went on to become Liverpool FC's most successful manager between 1974 and 1983, was all about. "This club has been my life," he once said. "I would go out and sweep the street and be proud to do it for Liverpool FC if they asked me to." Bob Paisley was never asked to do that, but he did sweep up plenty of silverware and who knows…maybe Jürgen will one day also be cast in bronze giving a trademark Klopp hug or fist-pump.

PUTTING IT ALL ON THE LINE

Kevin Keegan. Kenny Dalglish. Peter Beardsley. Steve McManaman. Luis Suarez. The Liverpool no.7 shirt has been worn by some exceptional players over the years, yet none have been in the mould of James Milner. A winger who arrived at Anfield in 2015 to play as a central midfielder, Milner has operated across the midfield, played in both full-back positions, skippered the Reds on almost a century of occasions despite never being club captain, scored crucial penalties, set a new Champions League assists record for a single season and is viewed as such a leader in the dressing room that he's almost a player-coach without the title. He does have a Premier League title and five other major honours to his name as a Red though. Trying to quantify the value of having Milner at LFC is almost impossible to do, but if one incident sums up his contribution it came against Bournemouth at Anfield in March 2020. Liverpool were en route to winning a first league title for 30 years, but after 18 consecutive wins had surprisingly been beaten 3-0 at Watford the week before. When Bournemouth netted early on at Anfield, nerves started to jangle before Mo Salah and Sadio Mane put the Redmen ahead. But in the second half, Ryan Fraser lobbed the ball over Adrian for a certain equaliser until Milner – captaining Liverpool and playing at left-back – raced back to the goalline and cleared the danger with a sliding volley. Liverpool went on to win 2-1, setting a new record of 22 consecutive top-flight home wins, and the versatile Milner had once again made a crucial contribution in the famous no.7 shirt.

I FEEL FINE

I FEEL FINE

FROM BOOM TO ZOOM

On Friday 13 March 2020, as the world faced up to the COVID-19 pandemic, Premier League football was suspended. For Liverpool supporters, a time of great uncertainty was accentuated by the fact the Reds were top of the league and needed just six more points to be champions for the first time since 1990. Such an outcome was plunged into doubt. Ten days later, the United Kingdom went into lockdown. Workplaces, schools and non-essential shops and businesses were closed. Citizens could only leave their homes for one hour of outside exercise per day. During such unprecedented times, people look towards leaders. For followers of Liverpool, that meant looking towards Jürgen Klopp. He immediately issued an open letter to supporters which included the following: "We don't want games or competitions suspended, but if doing so helps one individual stay healthy – just one – we do it no questions asked." Over the weeks and months that followed the Reds' boss gave a series of video interviews and updates with fans also given access to footage of the players meeting on Zoom for home workouts and training sessions. Somehow, Klopp always seems to be able to find the right words to say in any given situation and a fortnight after football was suspended he managed to again, despite the extraordinary circumstances. "Football is not the most important thing in the world," he said. "One hundred per cent not. In this moment it's clear what is. But the only way to get football back as soon as possible, if that's what the people want, the more disciplined we are now the earlier we will get, piece by piece by piece, our life back. That's how it is. There is no other solution in the moment, nobody has another solution. We have to be disciplined by ourselves, we have to keep the distance to other people. We have to give our people in the hospitals, our doctors, the chance to treat the people with serious issues with full concentration. We have to give people time to build ventilators, we have to give people time to find solutions. There will be a moment when other smart people find a vaccine for the virus. But until then, we have to make sure we do the best possible for all the people out there. In a lot of parts of my life football is my first concern, but not in this moment and I want to make sure that people know that and maybe they can see it in the same way." The sacrifices our health workers made during this awful period, and those we sadly lost during the pandemic, remain in our thoughts and during lockdown Klopp and his players also relased a video [pictured] thanking our NHS and healthworker heroes for their remarkable dedication, care and commitment during the most difficult of times.

 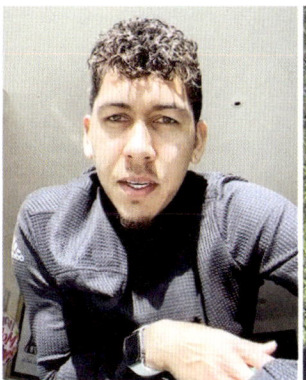  

53
CRYSTAL BALL

Even if Liverpool had lost all nine of their matches when football resumed in June 2020 following a three-month suspension due to the COVID-19 pandemic, they would have still been Premier League champions. The 82 points the Reds had accumulated before football was halted was one more than runners-up Manchester City managed when the season concluded in July, but who wants to win the league on the back of multiple defeats? Liverpool certainly didn't and after restarting with a 0-0 draw at Everton, the Reds took Crystal Palace apart in their first game back at Anfield, albeit with no supporters inside. "The fans haven't disappeared, they're just somewhere else," wrote Jordan Henderson in his matchday programme notes. Trent Alexander-Arnold's free-kick and Mo Salah's finish – the Reds' 100th goal of the season – ensured a 2-0 half-time lead before Fabinho scored the pick of the goals with a long-range thunderbolt. Sadio Mane added a fourth and when the full-time whistle blew, the stats showed that Roy Hodgson's Eagles hadn't touched the ball once in the Liverpool penalty area, a Premier League first since records began. And a first Premier League title for Liverpool was to follow just 24 hours later...

I FEEL FINE

54
SHOW ME LOVE

I FEEL FINE

If Manchester City didn't win at Chelsea, Liverpool would be 2019/20 Premier League champions with seven games of the season to play. So Jürgen Klopp told all in the 'Melwood bubble' to report to Formby Hall Golf Resort that evening for a barbeque and to watch their title rivals. With 12 minutes to go, and the Stamford Bridge score at 1-1, Fernandinho was sent off for handball on the goalline and Willian stepped up to score the penalty that confirmed Liverpool FC were English champions for the first time in 30 years. Klopp and his players partied, throwing out shapes to dance classics such as *Show Me Love* and *Freed From Desire* in their Liverpool shirts, and the following day the Reds' boss reflected on the scale of the achievement. "I thought a lot about what we did in the last few years and I think one of the most important things I said – I had no idea how important this was when I said it – was we have to write our own story and create our own history. Because that's what was necessary and that's what these boys have done now." History will recall them as legends.

I FEEL FINE

v Manchester City	Etihad Stadium
v Aston Villa	Anfield
v Brighton & Hove Albion	AMEX Stadium
v Burnley	Anfield
v Arsenal	Emirates Stadium
v Chelsea	Anfield
v Newcastle United	St James' Park

I FEEL FINE

SEVEN GUARDS OF HONOUR

Never before had a team from the English top flight won the league title with seven games to spare – but that's exactly what Jürgen Klopp's Reds did during season 2019/20. The disruption due to the COVID-19 pandemic meant that the title success wasn't confirmed until late June, but such was Liverpool's dominance that seven opposition teams followed modern protocol and formed a guard of honour to welcome the Reds onto the pitch for their remaining fixtures. Deposed champions Manchester City were the first to do so, followed by Aston Villa, Brighton, Burnley, Arsenal, Chelsea and Newcastle United.

PIONS

I FEEL FINE

"That's how life is, you make the best of what you get," said Jürgen Klopp when asked by Sky Sports' Kelly Cates about lifting the Premier League trophy behind closed doors at Anfield. After a 30-year wait for a league title it wasn't the evening everyone had hoped it would be, but after beating Chelsea 5-3, the Reds made the best of the situation under the circumstances. A podium was constructed on the Kop, the pulsing heartbeat of Liverpool Football Club, and it was Sir Kenny Dalglish – LFC's last title-winning manager – who had the job of handing the Premier League trophy over. Klopp was the first to have a golden Premier League winners' medal hung around his neck by King Kenny, followed by the 23 players who had made enough appearances to qualify for such a prized possession. Finally, amidst the smoke and red lighting, Jordan Henderson emerged and was handed the trophy. He gave it a kiss, walked over to his team-mates, shuffled his feet and turned towards the hallowed Anfield turf before raising the gleaming silver, red-ribboned, golden-crowned trophy aloft as fireworks lit up the sky and a monsoon of ticker tape rained down. "I was never on the Kop before, it was pretty special," said Klopp. "I think it makes sense in the moment when people are not in that we use the Kop to celebrate it with them together in our hearts."

I FEEL FINE

"INCREDIBLE GOALS, SUPER FOOTBALL IN MOMENTS AND I LOVED THE GAME SO WE COULD ENJOY SO FAR, AND WILL ENJOY THE REST OF THE NIGHT"
– JÜRGEN KLOPP

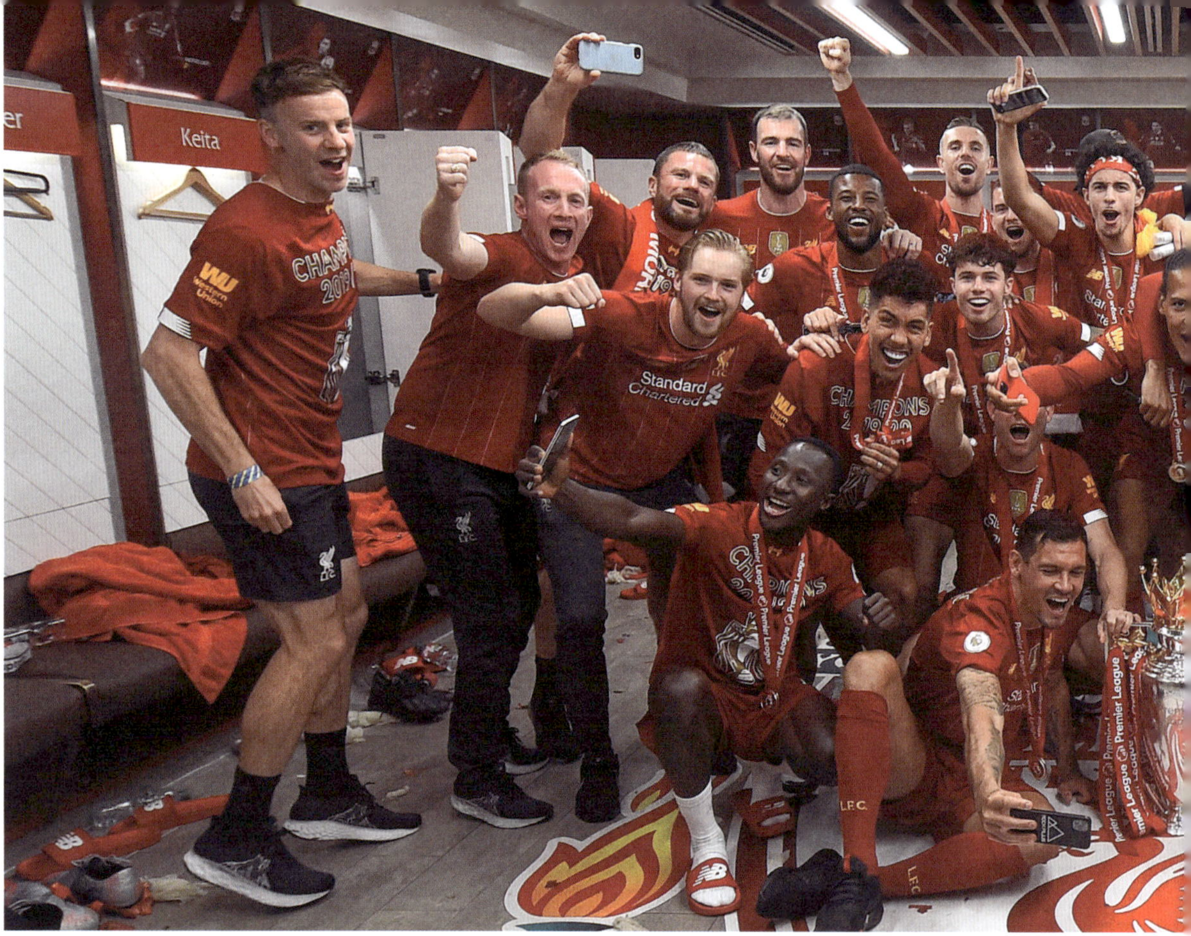
Keita
Standard Chartered

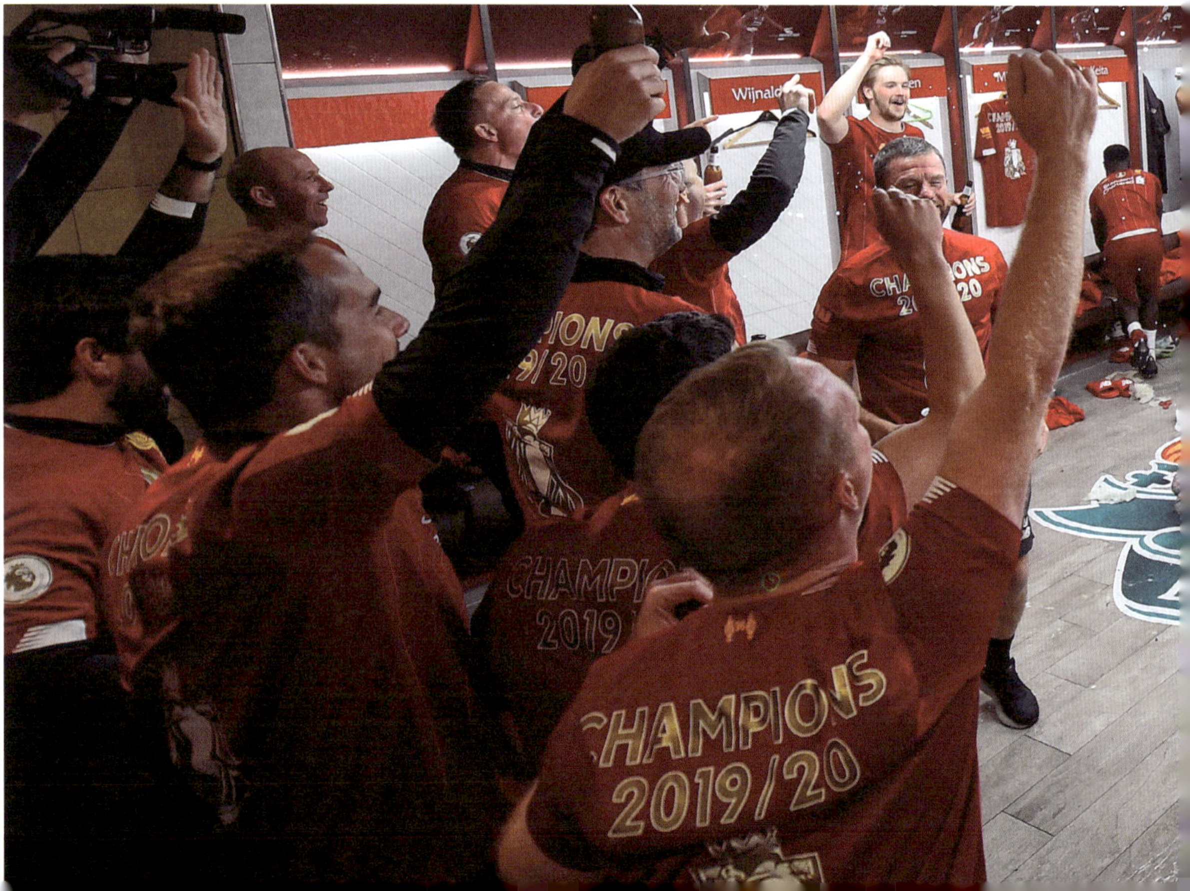
CHAMPIONS
2019/20

"THE TROPHY IS QUITE HEAVY, BUT WHEN YOU'VE GOT THE ADRENALINE RUNNING THROUGH YOU AND THE EMOTION, IT'S AS LIGHT AS A FEATHER"

– JORDAN HENDERSON

HOME IS WHERE THE ART IS

All around the streets of Anfield Road you'll find one of the finest collections of sporting art anywhere in the world. Thanks to talented artists using spray-painting and stencilling techniques, Liverpool players past and present have appeared on the walls of houses and businesses, effectively creating a free outdoor gallery. In the summer of 2019, after the Reds won a sixth European Cup, The Anfield Wrap commissioned a Trent Alexander-Arnold mural. Created by artist Akse, and situated on the corner of Sybil Road and Anfield Road, it features a quote from the Reds right-back: "I'm just a normal lad from Liverpool, whose dream has come true." A year later, on the same road, Redmen TV commissioned MurWalls to create a long-awaited glorious mural of Jordan Henderson lifting the Premier League trophy. Alongside it is another of MurWalls' finest pieces of work – legends Ian St John and Roger Hunt. The Saint signed the artwork in November 2020 before both he and Sir Roger joined Bill Shankly's Heaven XI in 2021. Ray Clemence is another much-missed Red to feature on a MurWalls mural, located on Wylva Road, while the same team of artists also painted legends Steven Gerrard and Alan Kennedy on Dinorwic Road and, in May 2022, unveiled a magnificent Ian Rush mural on Alroy Road, opposite Anfield's Main Stand. "To be so close to Anfield is amazing, it's a great honour. It's probably to scare the opposition!" said Rushie. A mural of Jürgen Klopp, created by John Culshaw, can be found on Houlding Street and the same artist is responsible for the striking image of Mo Salah that appeared opposite the King Harry pub on Anfield Road in 2022. There is also a poignant mural in tribute to Hillsborough campaigner Anne Williams – mum of Kevin, one of the 97 we lost in 1989 – on Sunbury Road. "Anne is someone the city can be proud of," said artist Paul Curtis. "She's the right sort of person to have a mural."

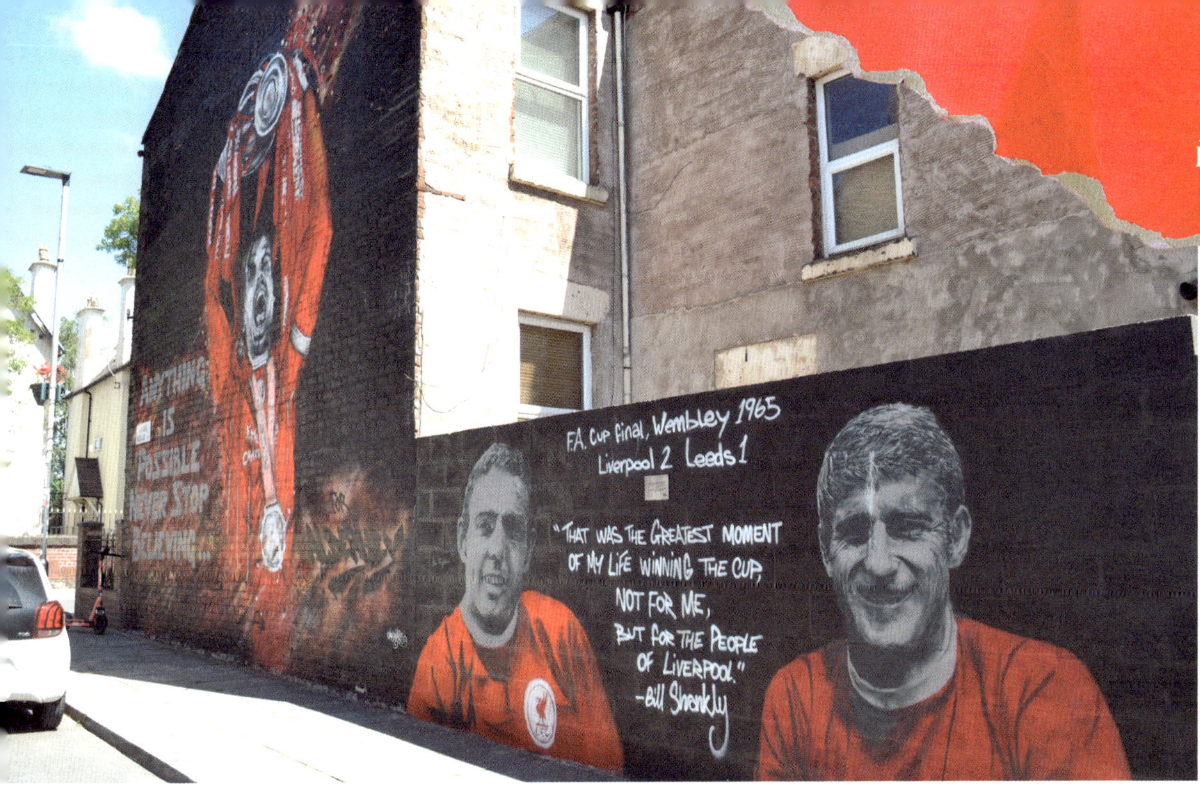
ANYTHING IS POSSIBLE NEVER STOP BELIEVING...
F.A. Cup Final, Wembley 1965
Liverpool 2 Leeds 1
"THAT WAS THE GREATEST MOMENT OF MY LIFE WINNING THE CUP, NOT FOR ME, BUT FOR THE PEOPLE OF LIVERPOOL."
-Bill Shankly

ALEXANDER-ARNOLD
66
'I'M JUST A NORMAL LAD FROM LIVERPOOL WHOSE DREAM HAS JUST COME TRUE'

"RAY HAD EVERYTHING. HE'S QUICK HE DOESN'T WANNA BE BEATEN. HE'S JUST A GREAT GOALKEEPER"
-Bill Shankly
APPEARANCES
665

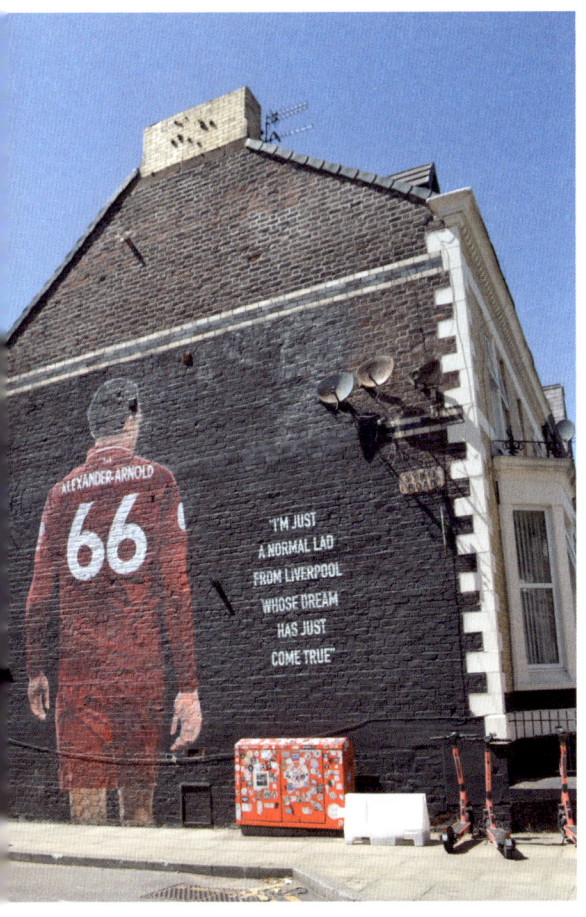

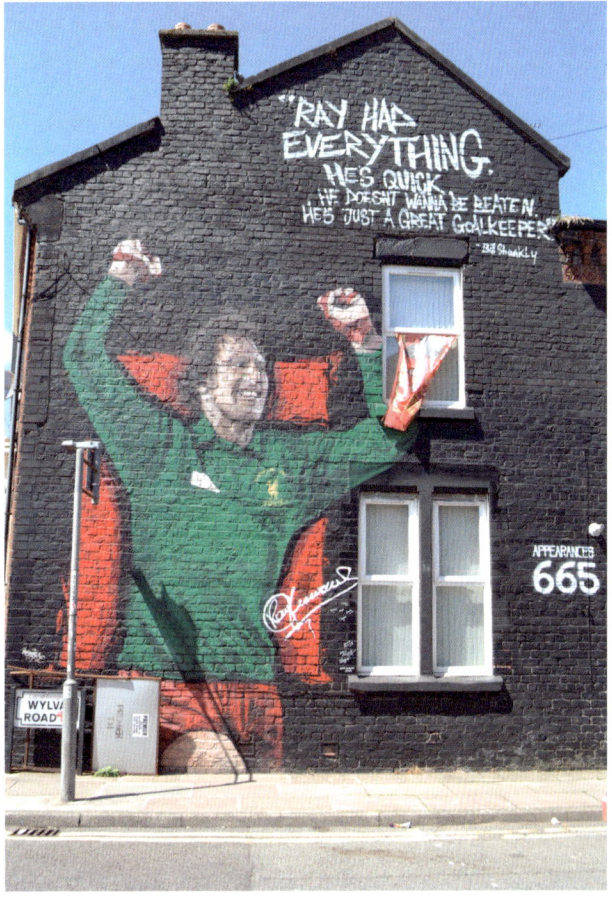

58 REDS SUPPORTING FOOD BANKS

Founded in October 2015, the same month that Jürgen Klopp was appointed as Liverpool FC manager, Fans Supporting Food Banks is a joint initiative between Reds' supporters union Spirit of Shankly and Everton's Blue Union. "What started with three fans collecting tins of food in a wheelie bin outside the pub on match days now supplies 25% of all donations to North Liverpool Food Banks," says Spirit of Shankly. "It has become a grassroots organisation that stretches from Glasgow to London to Dublin." The reality that hunger doesn't wear club colours has led to links being forged with supporters of many other clubs. For instance, Leicester City's Foxes Trust made donations before the two sides met at Anfield in February 2022. Liverpool FC's Red Neighbours community programme has also been prominent in tackling food poverty in the Anfield area – before, during and after coronavirus restrictions – while captain Jordan Henderson has used his matchday programme column on several occasions to highlight the need for food donations. Andy Robertson has been supporting food banks in his native Glasgow since before he was a Liverpool player and in July 2022, amidst a growing cost of living crisis, Robbo backed a Scottish Mail campaign to give every child in Scotland free school meals. "I don't think anyone should be going hungry, so the fact is if people are coming to school with no food, then we need to try to get these people fed – that's so important," said the Scotland skipper. "I'm based in Liverpool and I know the food bank numbers in Liverpool went through the roof during the pandemic. Nobody wants food banks because, if there's no food banks, it means everyone is getting fed but, unfortunately, just now we need them and a lot of families rely on them. It's up to everyone who can to help to try to ensure the number of these food banks goes down as we come out of the pandemic and try to get people in a better place financially. I feel as if we are a bit far away from that."

59
HAPPY BIRTHDAY TO YOU

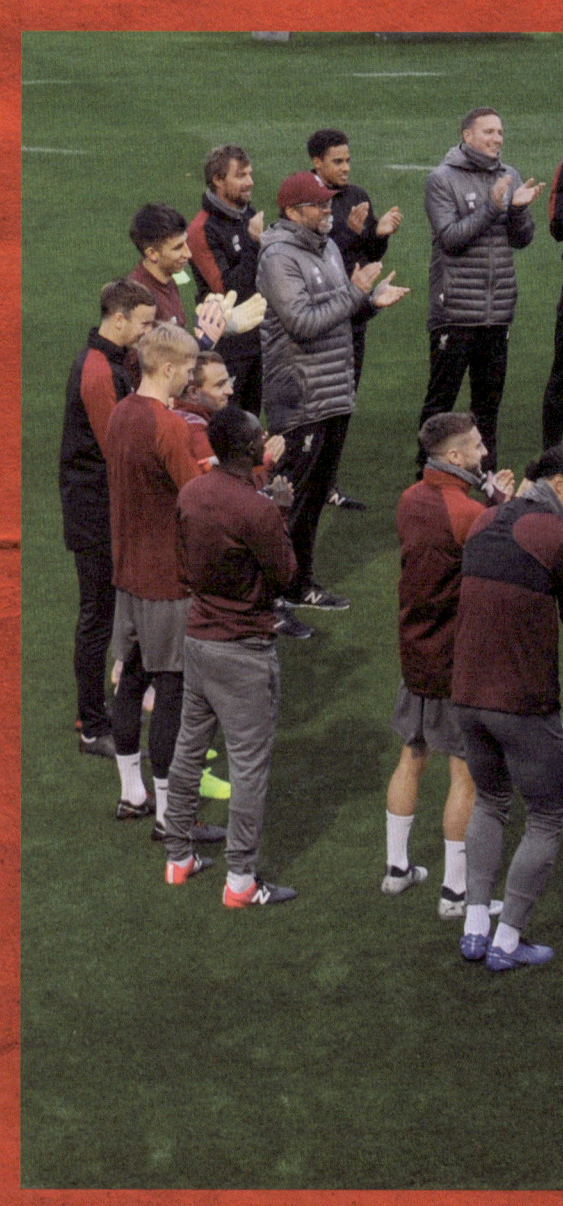

Successful teams have a strong team spirit and while the personalities involved are inevitably the most significant factor in how a group bonds, the way players are coached and managed is also crucial. It may only seem like a little thing, maybe insignificant to some, but if a Liverpool player's birthday falls on the day of a training session then his team-mates must be prepared to sing. Birthdays are marked by Jürgen Klopp, his first-team staff and players gathering in a circle before training and singing Happy Birthday To You in every language represented by the squad. It's done for fun, but also means all of the lads learn a few words of every team-mate's native language. Sometimes that's all you need for a bit of banter. While Happy Birthday To You is being sung in English, Dutch, German, French, Portuguese, Egyptian, Greek, Scouse and whatever other languages are spoken at the time, the rest of the lads clap along. Even Academy players invited to first-team training sessions have to join in, and only when the birthday boy has been sung to multiple times in multiple languages does the singing stop and the training start. You can also take it as Red that with guitar-strumming Alisson and piano-playing Roberto Firmino sharing a birthday on 2 October, it's a day when all the lads have to be in good voice!

60
HAT-TRICK HUNTERS!

Up until the summer of 2022 Jürgen Klopp had seen 10 hat-tricks scored by Liverpool players under his leadership. Interestingly, more than half of them had come away from Anfield. The first treble came from Divock Origi, who scored three in a 6-1 League Cup win at St Mary's in 2015. We had to wait another two years for the next one as Philippe Coutinho did the most damage in a 7-0 Champions League win against Spartak Moscow. A couple of months later, Porto were another European victim as Sadio Mane headlined the 5-0 win at Estadio do Dragao. It will probably surprise no-one to hear that Mo Salah has scored the most hat-tricks of the Klopp era with four. The most memorable came at Old Trafford in 2021 but he also claimed match balls against Leeds – in the opening league game of the 2020/21 season – and Bournemouth, and hit four against Watford at Anfield in 2018. Roberto Firmino is the first Brazilian to score two Premier League hat-tricks, doing so against Arsenal and Watford, while Diogo Jota's treble stunned Atalanta in the Champions League with the Reds winning 5-0.

I FEEL FINE

First 10 hat-tricks of the Klopp era

Divock Origi	2 December 2015	v Southampton
Philippe Coutinho	6 December 2017	v Spartak Moscow
Sadio Mane	14 February 2018	v Porto
Mohamed Salah (4)	17 March 2018	v Watford
Mohamed Salah	8 December 2018	v Bournemouth
Roberto Firmino	29 December 2018	v Arsenal
Mohamed Salah	12 September 2020	v Leeds United
Diogo Jota	3 November 2020	v Atalanta
Roberto Firmino	16 October 2021	v Watford
Mohamed Salah	24 October 2021	v Manchester Utd

I FEEL FINE

I FEEL FINE

61

10,000 & COUNTING

A goal which brings up such a big landmark deserves a greater audience, but Diogo Jota's simple finish to score the Reds' 10,000th goal in club history was played out in front of a COVID-affected fan-free Anfield in October 2020. The occasion was a Champions League group stage match against FC Midtjylland and Jota broke the deadlock in the 55th minute after great work from Xherdan Shaqiri and Trent Alexander-Arnold down the right saw the latter square the ball across the six-yard box for the Portuguese to guide home. Jota took the acclaim with an arms-folded celebration in front of an empty Kop, but a passionate, knowledgeable Anfield crowd would have loved a milestone moment like this. For the record, goal 10,001 was a Mo Salah penalty that sealed the 2-0 win.

I FEEL FINE

Milestone LFC goals

1: Jock Smith v Higher Walton 03.09.1892
1,000: Sam Raybould v Aston Villa 24.11.1906
2,000: Cyril Oxley v Newcastle United 25.12.1925
3,000: Jack Balmer v Aston Villa 15.10.1938
4,000: Jimmy Melia v Leyton Orient 08.11.1958
5,000: Ian St John v Watford 03.09.1969
6,000: Terry McDermott v West Ham 09.08.1980
7,000: John Aldridge v Tottenham 26.03.1989
8,000: Michael Owen v Southampton 26.08.2000
9,000: Sotirios Kyrgiakos v Blackpool 03.10.2010
10,000: Diogo Jota v FC Midtjylland 27.10.2020

PERFECT FACILITIES

After 70 years of training at Melwood, Liverpool FC moved to a new training base on the same site as the Academy in 2020. The AXA Training Centre was built on 9,200 square metres of land in Kirkby and features three full-size football pitches plus a special training area for the goalkeepers and a warm-up zone. It took 722 days to build and also includes a 30m x 30m Astroturf pitch, a tennis court and a padel tennis court. A keen padel tennis player himself, Jürgen Klopp's office overlooks the pitches and not far from it are replicas of the FIFA Club World Cup, UEFA Super Cup, UEFA Cup, European Cup, Premier League trophy, Football League Championship Trophy, FA Cup and League Cup housed in glass cases, with the number of times the Reds have won each of them displayed underneath. There's also a state-of-the-art gym, rehab gym, hydrotherapy area including a heated swimming pool, jacuzzi, sauna and hot and cold pools, plus a full-size, multi-use indoor sports hall, which includes 5-a-side goals, basketball hoops and a giant screen. Add to that an impressive atrium featuring The Champions Wall, a nicely designed dining area, a media suite and large players' changing room with individual PIN code lockers and it's no wonder that Klopp is so happy with LFC's modern training base. "It is a wonderful building," he said. "You have everything you need for now and for the future. It's a great place to be and the pitches are outstanding. We have perfect facilities here. Kirkby will never be an excuse for any game we lose in the future."

I FEEL FINE

BACK ON OUR PERCH
LFC AUSTIN
JUSTICE FOR THE 96
NEVER FORGOTTEN
Liverpool FC

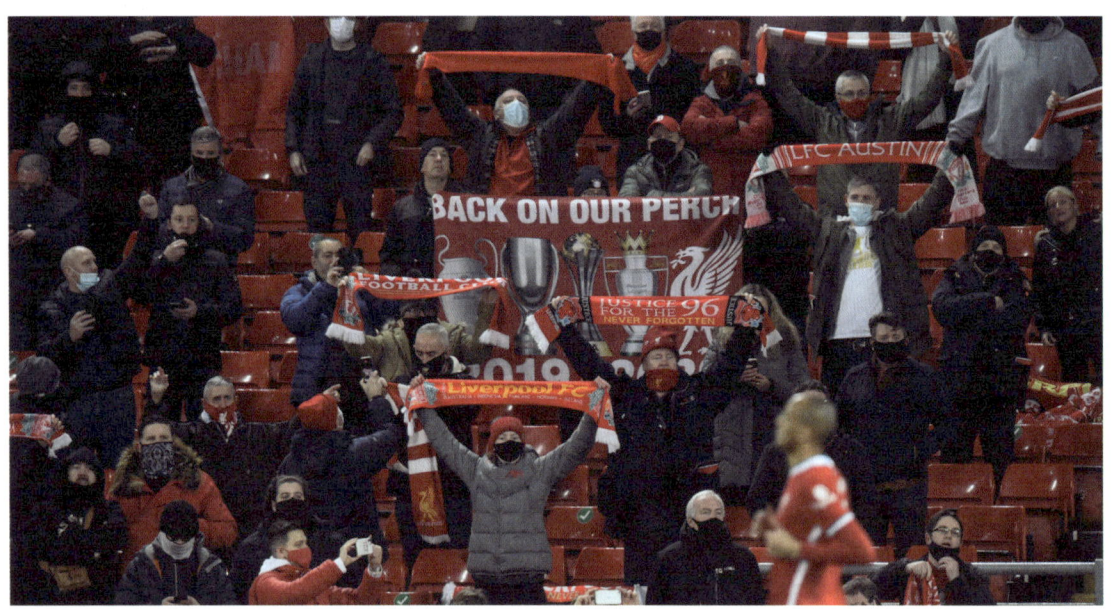

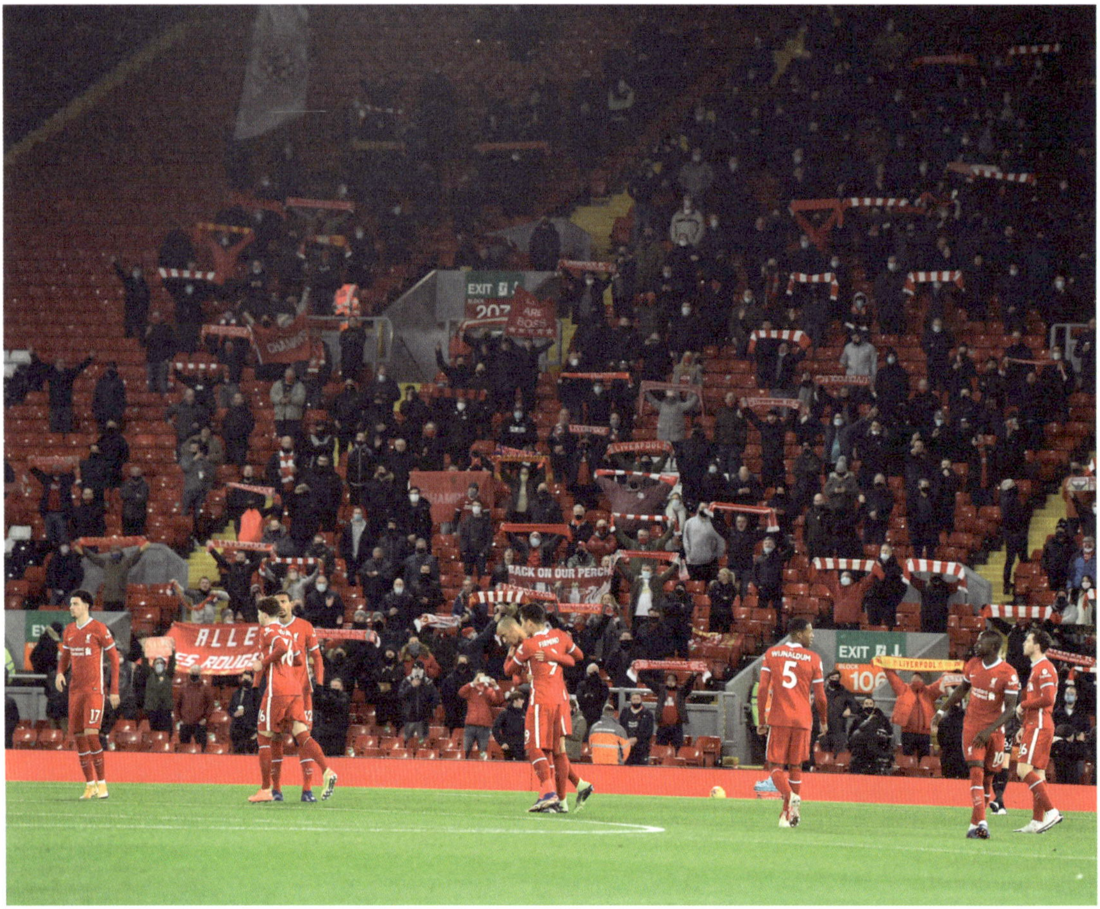
BACK ON OUR PERCH
EXIT
WIJNALDUM
5

63
THIS IS PANFIELD

Truth be told, season 2020/21 is largely best forgotten. Liverpool suffered an unprecedented injury crisis, were on the end of some baffling VAR decisions, had to play a 'home' Champions League game in Budapest and endured a terrible run of form in early 2021 that included a dispiriting six consecutive Anfield Premier League defeats, having lost none of the previous 68. Worst of all, the vast majority of the season was played behind closed doors as the COVID-19 pandemic continued to disrupt normal ways of life. In December 2020, however, there was a brief respite from the gloom for a handful of match-going Reds when Anfield was allowed to host 2,000 socially-distanced, mask-wearing supporters for three Premier League games. After ending a second national lockdown, the government announced a new system of tiered restrictions. The city of Liverpool was placed in tier 2 and under the rules a couple of thousand ballot-winning Reds returned to Anfield in early December to see Jürgen Klopp's men beat Wolves 4-0. Joel Matip was among the goalscorers in what ended up being Liverpool's biggest home win of the season – which was no coincidence. "I think it's a huge difference," said Wolves defender Leander Dendoncker afterwards. "It felt like there were at least 15,000 people in here when you heard the noise. They managed to push their team forward." Another 2,000 Reds were inside Anfield 10 days later to see Spurs beaten 2-1, Roberto Firmino netting a late winner, but a disappointing 1-1 draw against West Bromwich Albion between Christmas and New Year was the last game to be played in front of any sort of an Anfield crowd until May. Another national lockdown was announced by the government in early January and with Anfield once again empty, the champions took just one point from the next 21 available at their unmanned fortress.

64
RHYS & NAT

Liverpool's place in the 2022 Champions League final was secured with a 3-2 comeback victory in Villarreal. Substitute Luis Diaz deservedly earned the plaudits for his brilliant second-half display, but after seeing his side win at El Madrigal, the thoughts of Jürgen Klopp were elsewhere. "I messaged Rhys Williams and Nat Phillips because we wouldn't be there without them," he revealed. "I remember the final game of last season and they left the pitch with a bandage around the head, cuts on their faces, and that was really a symbol for the whole period. We went through on one leg, with one eye…it was incredible. It was such a tough season." In mid-April 2021, with Fabinho and on-loan Ozan Kabak playing at centre-back due to long-term injuries to Virgil van Dijk, Joel Matip and Joe Gomez, Liverpool conceded late goals to draw 1-1 against Leeds United and Newcastle United. It left the Reds in sixth position, four points adrift of Champions League qualification, with five games to play. Klopp decided it was time to restore Fabinho to midfield and introduce a new, inexperienced central defensive partnership of Phillips and Williams. The pair had only played alongside each other once before, a 0-1 home defeat to Fulham in early March, but they rose to the challenge. Liverpool won all five of their remaining Premier League games, keeping three clean sheets, to not only secure Champions League qualification on the final day of the season against Crystal Palace, but finish in third place against all the odds. So when his side reached the Champions League final in Paris 12 months later, Klopp was keen to ensure that the unexpected roles Williams and Phillips played were recognised. "Hopefully nobody forgot how hard we fought to get here. We felt it mentally. The public wasn't shy of telling us that we underperformed and all these kinds of things. You try to understand, you think, 'Wait a minute, we're facing teams in the strongest league in the world having played for the majority of the time without our full defence.' We had no centre-halves, had to play midfielders in the last line, then had to use other players in midfield and nothing worked really. In the end, we played with two incredible players – Rhys and Nat – but we couldn't use them earlier because they needed time to adapt. So, yes, there was a bit of a point to prove and I'm really happy that the boys did that."

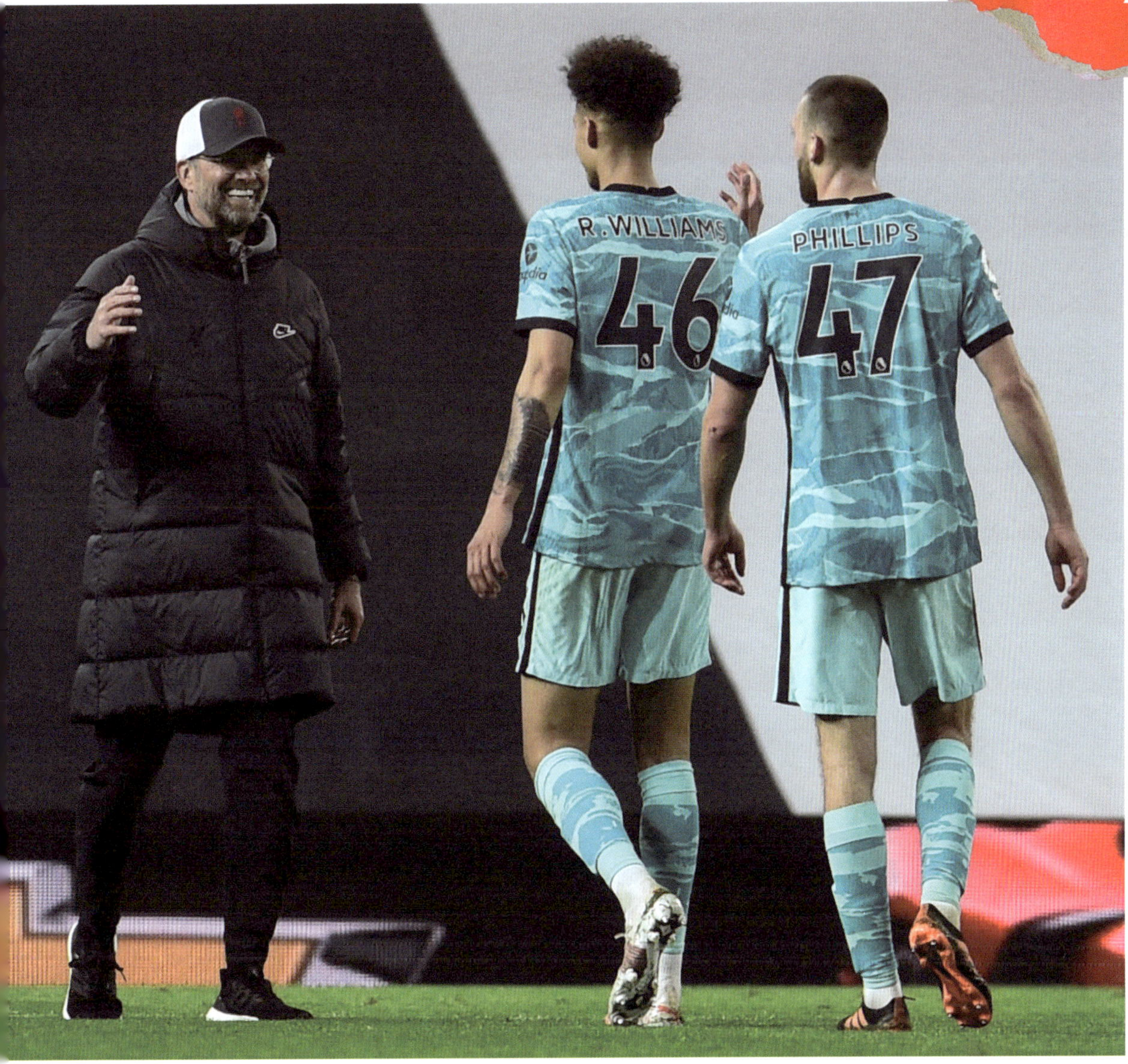
R.WILLIAMS
46
PHILLIPS
47

Standard Chartered
47

19

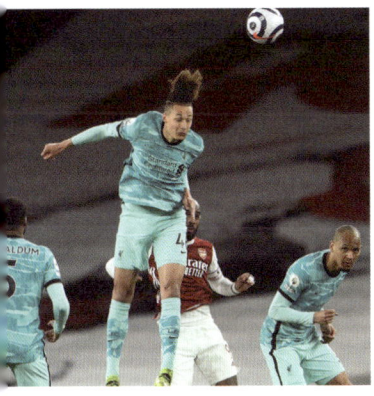

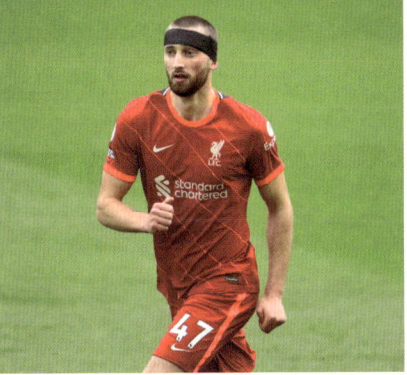

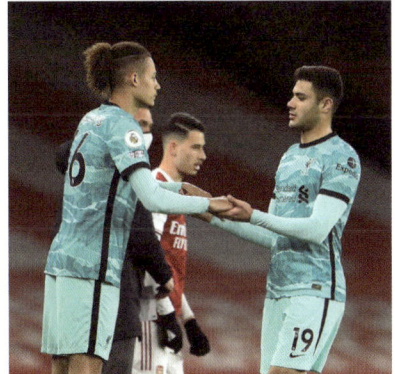

I FEEL FINE

65
HOLY GOALIE!

The Hawthorns holds a place in Liverpool's illustrious history as the venue where the Reds won their maiden First Division title in 1901. One hundred and twenty years later, West Bromwich Albion's home was the scene of perhaps the most remarkable goal ever scored by a Liverpool player. Sam Allardyce's already-relegated Baggies looked like they would hold Liverpool to a 1-1 draw. With just two Premier League games to play it would leave potential Champions League qualification out of the injury-ravaged Reds' hands, but then a guy who is good with his hands – goalkeeper Alisson – was sent forward for a 95th-minute corner by goalkeeping coach John Achterberg. No Liverpool goalie had ever scored during a competitive game in 129 years of football. No goalkeeper had ever scored a header in the Premier League. Alisson had never scored before either, so it seemed the best Kopites could hope for was that he'd distract the Albion defence to allow a team-mate to take advantage. But when Trent Alexander-Arnold's corner swung towards him, the Brazilian rose imperiously at the near post and turned his head in mid-air to guide a stunning, accurate, scarcely-believable header into the net, giving the Redmen a crucial last-ditch win. It was one of those 'did that really just happen?' moments and even Jürgen Klopp on the touchline momentarily looked unsure about how to celebrate. "It's an unbelievable header, I've never seen anything like that," said the Liverpool manager. Alisson, whose father Jose Agostinho Becker had tragically drowned in a Brazilian lake just three month earlier, celebrated his goal by pointing towards the heavens as he was mobbed by his joyous team-mates. He was understandably emotional in his post-match interview. "I'm too emotional these last months for everything that happened with me, with my family," he told Sky Sports. "But football is my life, I played since I remember with my father. I hope he was here to see it, but I'm sure that he's seeing with God on his side and celebrating. It's for my family, for the boys."

I FEEL FINE

66

Sometimes the smallest of details can lead to the biggest successes in football and Jürgen Klopp is a manager who leaves no stone unturned in the pursuit of success at Liverpool. Never afraid to innovate, Klopp brought in a throw-in coach in 2018 after reading about him in German newspaper BILD. Thomas Gronnemark, a former sprinter and member of Denmark's bobsleigh team, reinvented himself as the world's first throw-in coach in 2004, creating drills to improve technique, applying mathematics to design the best angles and height for players to receive a throw-in at, and coaching players on how to press from an opponents' throw-in. "I categorise throw-ins into three categories – long, fast and clever," he said. "With Liverpool, I work more on the fast and clever options, as they don't look to utilise the long throw into the box when in the final third." The benefits of working with Gronnemark are subtle but successful. Since being coached by the Dane, Andy Robertson can throw the ball

I FEEL FINE

LFC: LONG, FAST AND CLEVER

eight metres further while his routines have led to numerous goals for Liverpool. For instance, during the Reds' 2019/20 Premier League title success, the 2-1 win at Southampton in August 2019 came when the Reds scored from two throw-ins – one taken by Robertson and another when Sadio Mane won possession from a Saints throw-in. The season before, Mo Salah scored in home and away wins against Bournemouth from throw-in routines. Klopp innovated again during season 2021/22 when he brought in neuro11, a specialist German neuroscience team which works on mental strengthening processes in stressful football situations. Neuro11 worked with the players during pre-season, specifically on set-pieces and penalty kicks as with UEFA scrapping the away goals rule in the Champions League, Liverpool's coaching staff felt there was a higher probability of penalty shoot-outs so the players needed to prepare. As it happened, the Reds reached the Champions League final without needing spot-kicks, but won three domestic cup ties on penalties including the Carabao Cup quarter-final and final against Leicester City and Chelsea, and the FA Cup final against Chelsea. Liverpool took 24 penalties across those three games and converted 22 of them, lifting two pieces of silverware as a result, while both Caoimhin Kelleher and Alisson made saves. Further proof that sometimes the smallest of details can lead to the biggest of successes in football for those who innovate.

67

I FEEL FINE

I FEEL FINE

HILLSBOROUGH

Jürgen Klopp was a 21-year-old striker playing in a German amateur league when the Hillsborough disaster occurred on 15 April 1989. Klopp had signed for FC Viktoria Sindlingen – a Frankfurt-based club in Oberliga Hessen – for a €4,000 transfer fee in 1988 and in December of that year became a father for the first time when son Marc was born. He also scored four goals in a 6-0 win against former club Eintracht Frankfurt Amateure (now Eintracht Frankfurt II), but as the season headed towards its conclusion Viktoria Sindlingen were embroiled in a relegation battle. They faced a play-off against FC Erbach, and during it Klopp headed home his 14th and final goal of the season to put his side 3-2 up. They went on to win 4-2, avoiding relegation. It's a reminder that Jürgen could not have been much further removed from the events in Sheffield, where 97 Liverpool supporters were unlawfully killed, in 1989, yet you'd never know it. Since becoming LFC manager, he has educated himself on what happened and always speaks about it with care and understanding. Even so, for someone who was a 21-year-old new dad at the time, and whose first language is German, it cannot be an easy subject to naturally talk about. Which made the words he spoke on the 33rd anniversary of the Hillsborough disaster in April 2022 – the first since Andrew Devine had become the 97th victim – all the more special. "When speaking on this subject I am woefully inadequate to find words that properly reflect its significance. I try to leave that to others," he said. "But I know – because I talk to people who understand far better than me – that taking time to remember and reflect around this time is so important to the families of the victims and the survivors. For those who lost loved ones on that awful day, the pain will never diminish. For those who were there, who themselves were hurt or injured – or even witnessed the horror – they can never eradicate those feelings. So we must continue to support them and observe this anniversary in a manner which honours the memory of those we lost. But also acknowledge the courage, fortitude and resilience of the people who fought for justice in their memory for decades. The majority of us honoured to represent this club today can never truly comprehend the suffering, but we can express our love and our solidarity."

68

Back in 1996 a mosaic was organised and displayed for the first time on the Kop for a match against Manchester United. Originally the brainchild of supporter Andy Knott, a piece of card was placed on every seat in football's most famous stand for Kopites to hold up at a set time to create a spectacular mosaic displaying a key message. The dedication and commitment required to set up such a massive operation is indicative of how far fans will go to make this club stand out from the rest. Hillsborough anniversaries have prompted many mosaics, as have departing players and the deaths of legends. That mosaic tradition has continued through the Klopp era, with some even expanding to encompass other stands in the ground. A full-capacity Anfield at the start of the 2021/22 season gave the opportunity for fans to pay tribute to the 97th Hillsborough victim, Andrew Devine. The Villarreal Europa League semi-final tie in 2016 saw three sides of the ground form a powerful mosaic after the Hillsborough 'unlawfully killed' verdicts came through. A derby match was a fitting way to pay tribute to LFC legend Ronnie Moran, also affectionately known as 'Bugsy', after he died in 2017. The club's 125th anniversary, and what would have been Bob Paisley's 100th birthday, brought spectacular displays – and the first home Premier League game after the Reds won the European Cup for the sixth time in 2019 seemed a good time to show off Ol' Big Ears in card form!

MOSAICS

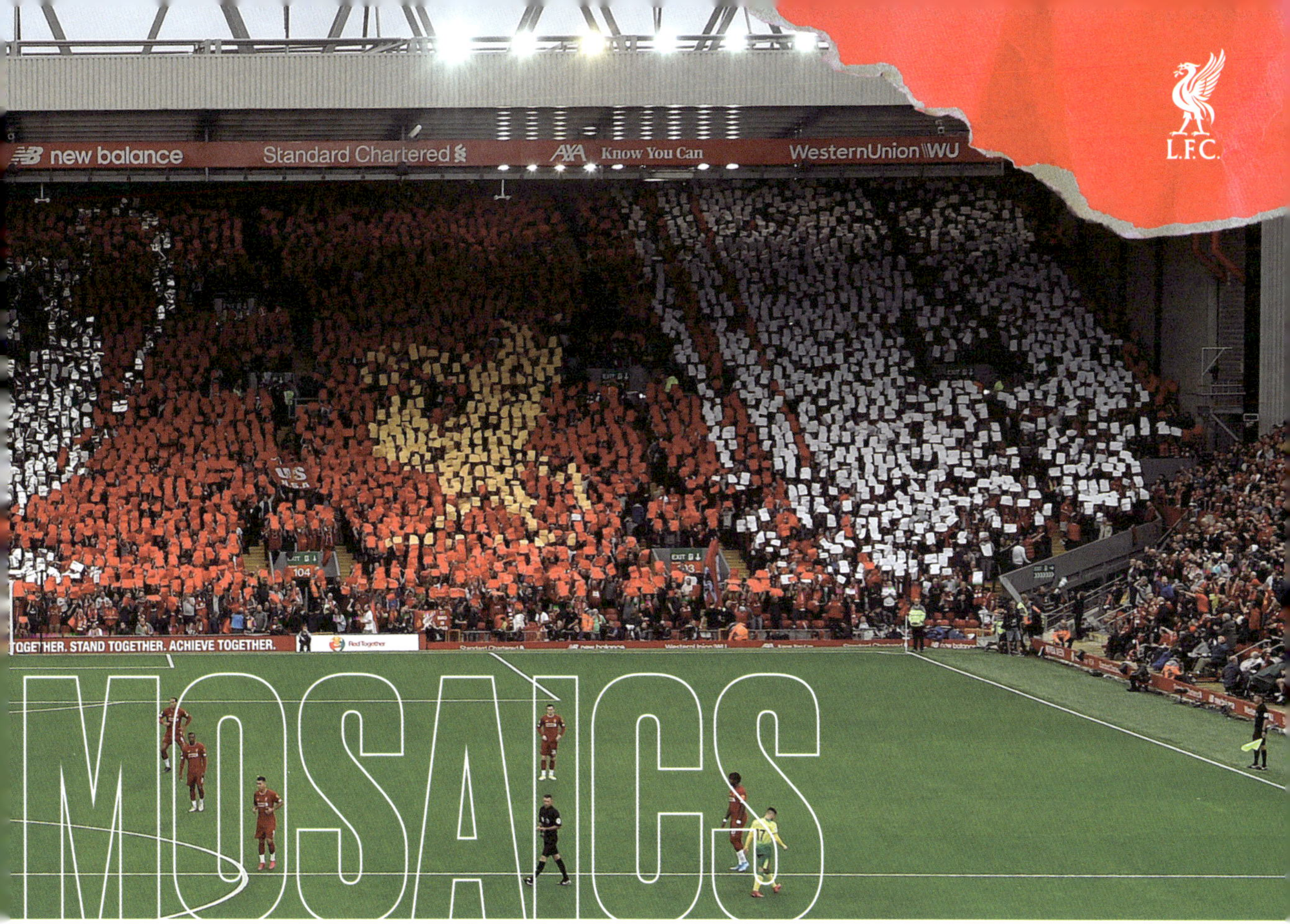
L.F.C.
new balance
Standard Chartered
AXA Know You Can
WesternUnion WU
TOGETHER. STAND TOGETHER. ACHIEVE TOGETHER.

BUGSY

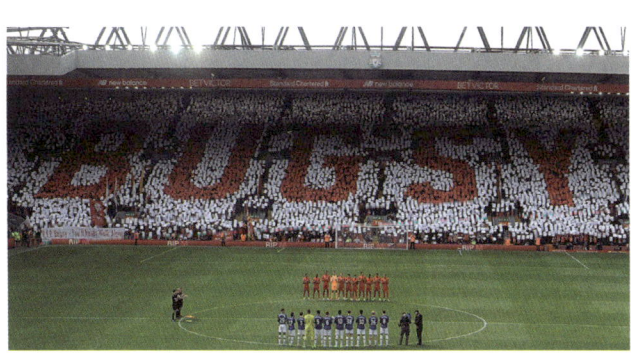

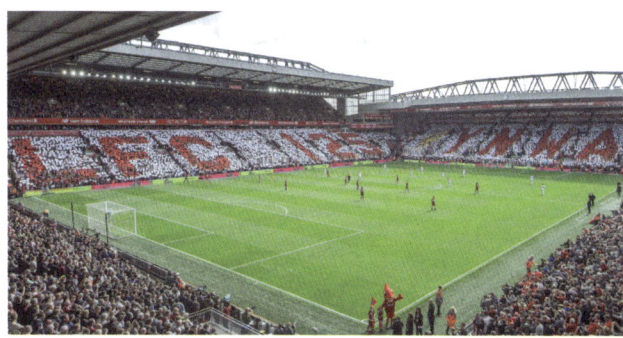

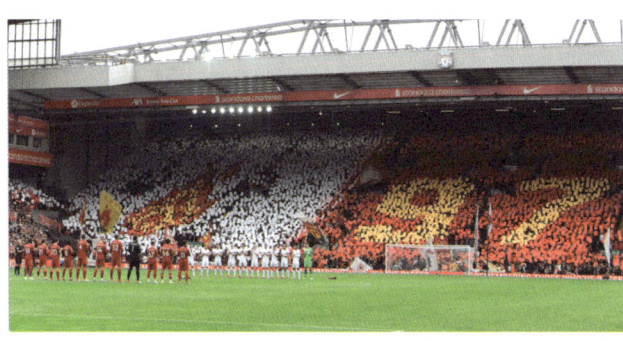

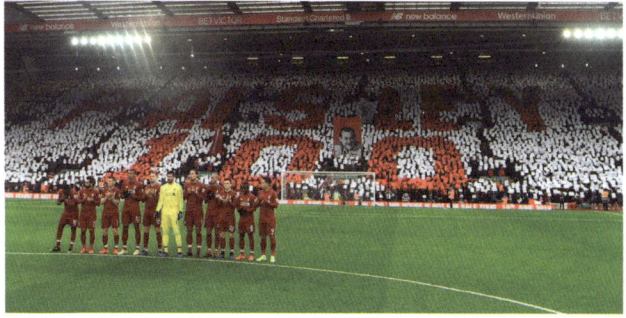

FOOTBALL IS BACK AND IT'S WONDERFUL

Some renditions of You'll Never Walk Alone are more emotional than others. The one before Liverpool versus Burnley in August 2021 didn't so much bring tears to the eyes as make them roll down cheeks. Finally, after 528 days, Anfield was full again. It felt more like a reunion than a Premier League match as Liverpool supporters caught up with friendly faces unseen for 17 months and paid tribute to those we lost along the way. Stadium announcer Peter McDowall read a long list of names of those who had passed. One of them was Andrew Devine, the 97th unlawfully killed victim of the Hillsborough disaster. A mosaic displaying '97' and the eternal flames was held aloft on the Kop after a spine-tingling YNWA. As captain Jordan Henderson placed a wreath behind the goal to thunderous applause, it only added to the heightened sense of emotion. Burnley had ended Liverpool's record-breaking 68-game unbeaten home league run at an empty Anfield seven months earlier. They'd had their day. This was ours. With the twelfth man behind them, and Virgil van Dijk back on the Anfield pitch after serious injury, Jürgen Klopp's Reds were back. Before the match, writing in the official matchday programme, Klopp expressed his delight at the prospect of seeing a full stadium again. "Good afternoon and welcome back to Anfield for our Premier League game against Burnley," he wrote. "You have no idea how good it feels to say that. Welcome back! And a full welcome. A full Anfield. With a full away support. Football is back and it's wonderful." The Liverpool boss also finished his programme notes in a similar vein. "Our 2021/22 journey is underway and we should enjoy every second of it. Not because we know we will have success or we expect it – but because we chase it together, as a collective. It feels like an adventure again and

that is a wonderful sensation after so long apart. Welcome back – we've missed you like crazy." Liverpool won 2-0, Diogo Jota and Sadio Mane on the scoresheet, and with a full Anfield behind them the Reds remained undefeated at home in the Premier League for the fourth time in five seasons. Don't ever let anyone tell you Liverpool supporters don't make a difference.

70
THE WARMEST OF EMBRACES

Along with his old glasses, his cap and his fist pump, a warm bear hug has become one of Jürgen Klopp's trademarks. There can't be many opposition Premier League opponents who don't look over enviously as the Reds boss paces towards his players, one by one, offering a beaming smile and a giant hug after the final whistle as he shows his appreciation for the effort his boys have put in. The smile gets a little wider and the embrace lasts a little longer if the Reds have just won a game, of course. Shortly after Klopp's arrival, he explained why he dishes out the hugs. "I'm really demanding to be honest, and I really want a lot of them. When you can really see how they fight, with the last drop of fuel in their machine...that's the most easy thing to do."

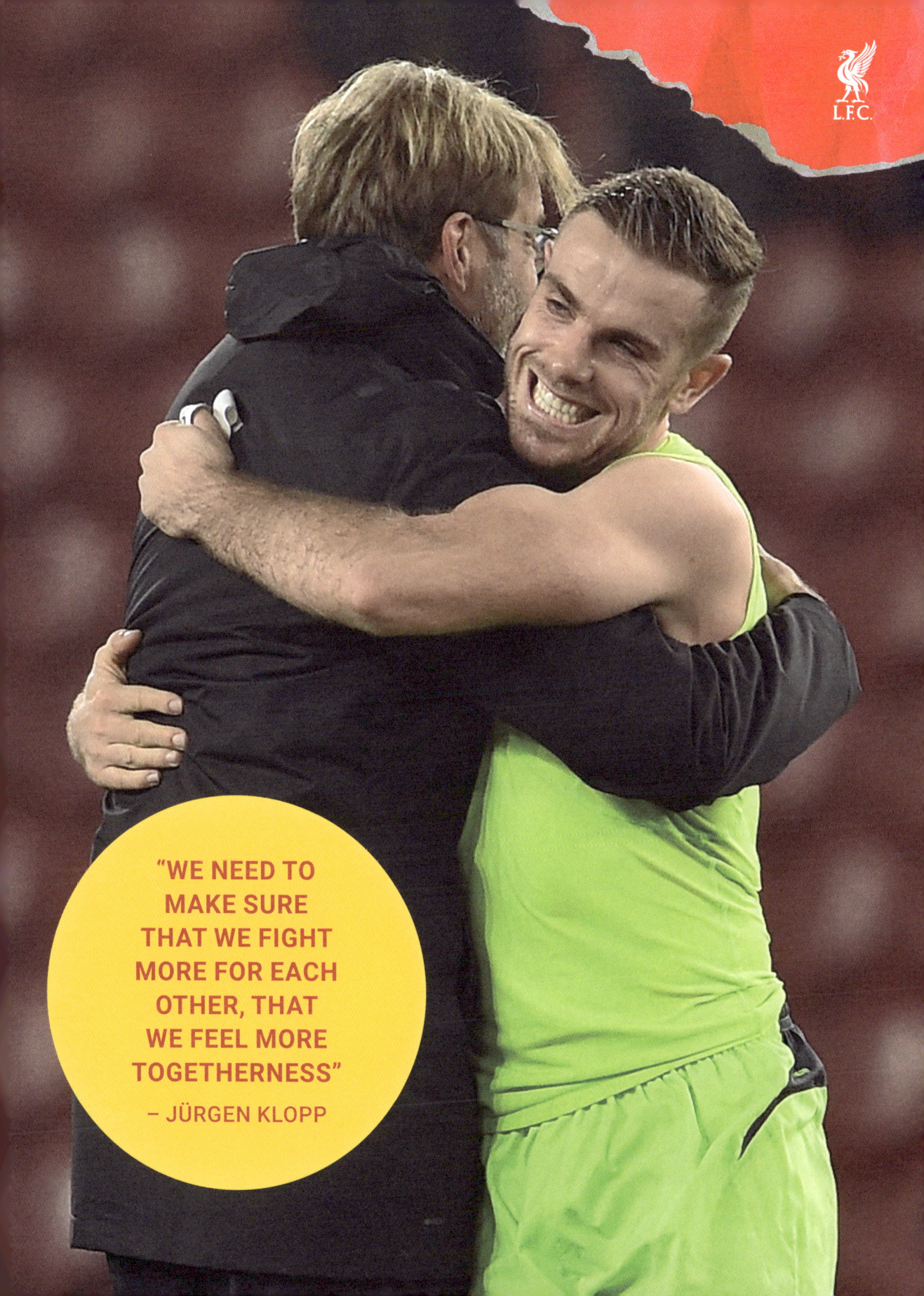

"HE GIVES EVERYONE HUGS. I LIKE HIM. HE'S SOMEONE WHO TREATS EVERYONE THE SAME"

– NABY KEITA

"AS A MANAGER, YOU NEED TO KNOW WHEN TO GIVE THE BEAR HUG AND WHEN TO GIVE THE BOOT UP THE BACKSIDE. HE JUDGES THAT PRETTY WELL"

– JAMES MILNER

71
DO IT AGAIN, MO!

For the first half of the 2021/22 season, in particular, Mo Salah was in sensational form. Up to and including his hat-trick at Old Trafford towards the end of October, the Egyptian King had scored 15 goals in his first 12 Liverpool matches of the season. But it wasn't just the sheer number of goals he was scoring that caught the eye – the quality of some of them was truly breathtaking. When Manchester City arrived at Anfield at the start of October, the league's heavyweights fought out a 2-2 draw but Salah's strike was the moment that made the biggest impression. Picking up the ball on his favourite right wing, he had three City players around him, but his close control saw him wriggle away, leaving Bernardo Silva on his backside. Facing Aymeric Laporte, he twisted one way and then the other to take the Spain international out of the equation before smashing a shot with his supposed weaker right foot across Ederson and into the far side netting. Such goals don't happen by fluke – but as if to remove any doubt whatsoever, he scored a goal of equal magic in the following Premier League match against Watford at Vicarage Road. With the Reds already three goals up, Salah took possession on the edge of the box and, surrounded by several defenders, he weaved a spell that saw him find space, before leaving another defender on the ground and whipping the ball into the far corner, this time with his favoured left foot. Bobby Firmino could feel a little disgruntled at the fact his hat-trick had been overshadowed by Salah's latest outstanding goal, but it was world class.

72

FOOTBALL HEAVEN

MANCHESTER UNITED 0 — 6:21
LIVERPOOL 5 — 0:00

Being a football fan can be difficult sometimes. The game can leave you feeling very low. Then there are afternoons like 24 October 2021 when almost everything just goes perfectly. In a season when the Reds beat their traditional rivals, Everton and Manchester United, both home and away for only the second time in the same campaign, the 5-0 victory at Old Trafford stands out – with the abiding memory being the vision of hundreds of United fans streaming out of the ground at half-time with the score already at 4-0. If the home side were shell shocked, Jürgen Klopp's men were clinical, and had the luxury of being able to coast through the final half hour of the match after Mo Salah had completed a fabulous hat-trick and Paul Pogba had been sent off. Naby Keita and Diogo Jota put the Reds two up after 15 minutes before the Mo Show began and the Reds finished with their second consecutive 5-0 away Premier League win, having beaten Watford by the same score the previous weekend. At times like this, football is a lot of fun.

AND THE HOME GAME WASN'T BAD EITHER...

In April the two sides met again and the Reds won 4-0 to take the aggregate score against Manchester United to 9-0 for the season. Mo Salah's double meant he became the first Liverpool player to score five league goals against United in the same season. Luis Diaz and Sadio Mane netted the Reds' other goals.

Premier League, 19 April 2022

Liverpool 4
Diaz (5)
Salah (22, 85)
Mane (68)

Man United 0

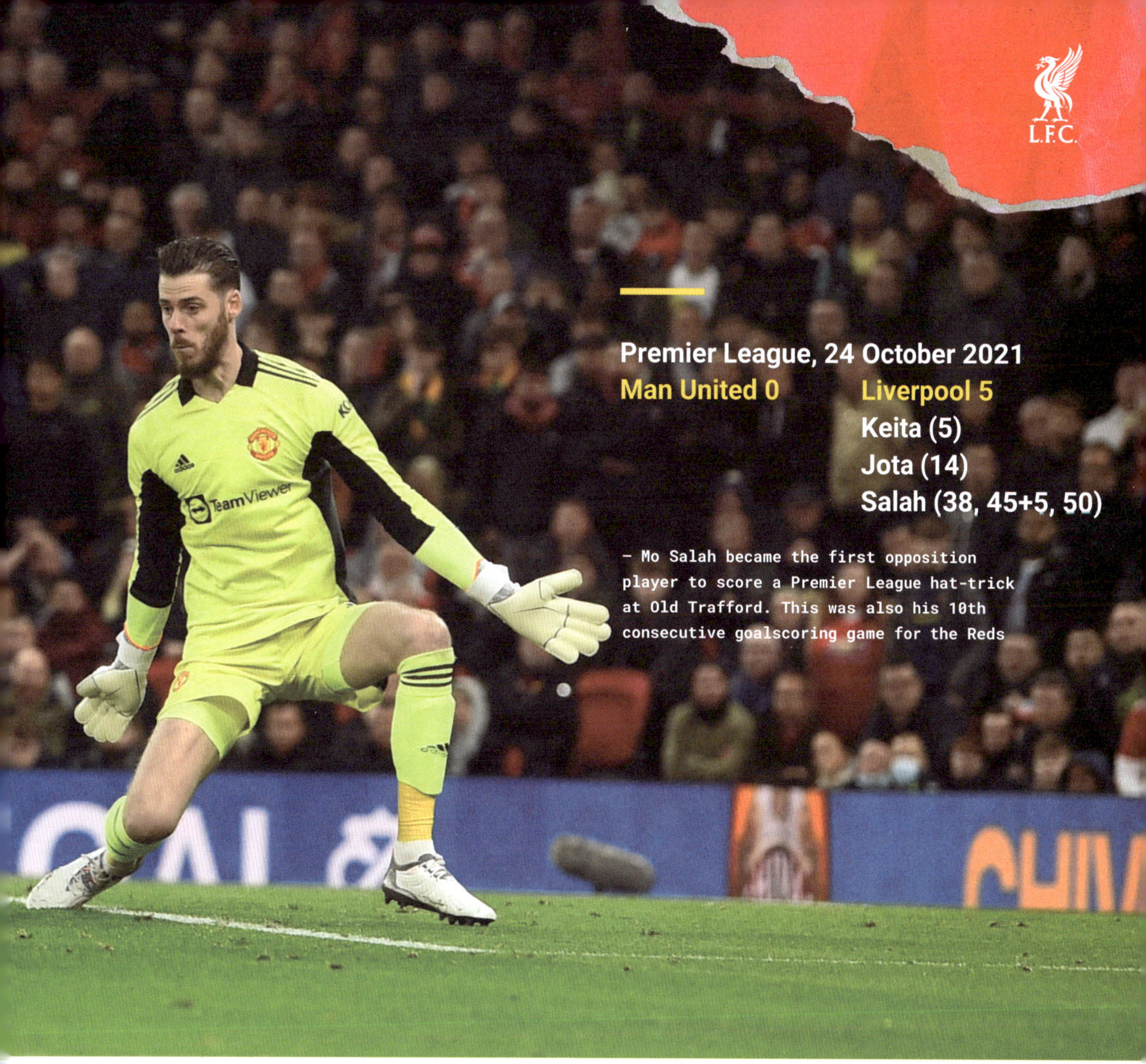

Premier League, 24 October 2021

Man United 0 **Liverpool 5**

Keita (5)
Jota (14)
Salah (38, 45+5, 50)

— Mo Salah became the first opposition player to score a Premier League hat-trick at Old Trafford. This was also his 10th consecutive goalscoring game for the Reds

LICENCE TO SKILL

73

Liverpool have had some talented technicians in recent years and every Kopite will have their own favourite. Some players are capable of audacious skills while others just ooze class every time they touch the ball. Think of Thiago, who not only spots passes no-one else can see, he also delivers them. With a drop of the shoulder and a wiggle of the hips, some say he could find space in a telephone box. Think of Luis Diaz, who found the time during a frenetic derby match to control a cross-field pass with his heel in mid-air. Think of Bobby Firmino with his no-look passes, Maradona turns and showreel of magic moments over the years. Think of Mo Salah and the unbelievable individual goals he's produced. And think of Divock Origi, whose improvisation saw him produce a scorpion-kick goal at Preston in October 2021. Just when you think you've seen it all, another Liverpool player will produce a moment of magic. With the current crop of stars, there are bound to be more to come.

I FEEL FINE

WELCOME BACK

If you do right by us, we'll do right by you. It could almost be a club motto. It's certainly how most fans feel about players and managers who have had a good career with the Reds and given everything they have for the cause. Even the best players and managers usually move on eventually, but as long as they don't do anything silly – like play for a major rival – they are normally guaranteed a great reception on their return to Anfield. Adam Lallana is one such example. He was a big part of recent successes but left the club during the COVID-19 pandemic, when there was no opportunity for supporters to show their affection. So when he was able to play in front of a packed Anfield for Brighton, there was a lot of love in the air. There's always a lot of love for club legend Steven Gerrard – even when he's in the opposition dugout. No matter who else he works for, everyone knows he's a Red to the core. Lots of players have left the club during Jürgen Klopp's long stint as manager and most are welcomed back with a hug from the boss and former colleagues – and applause from the stands. You're rarely forgotten if you've been one of the family at Anfield.

"He doesn't come here today for any sentiment or nostalgia. He comes to win. Of course, there will be an opportunity for our supporters to show love, respect and affection for a person who is rightly considered one of the all-time greats to ever wear a Liverpool shirt. But that is completely separate to the game. Steven is a serious guy. His commitment to Aston Villa today is absolute"

– **JÜRGEN KLOPP** ON STEVEN GERRARD (in his programme notes)

"Adam Lallana is our opponent today and we his. We want to beat him with all we have and he will feel the same about us. But I hope either side of the game there will be an opportunity for us all to show appreciation to Adam for his contribution. Adam is one of the founding fathers of the success this current Liverpool side has enjoyed in recent seasons and I personally will forever be grateful for what he did when with us"

– **JÜRGEN KLOPP** ON ADAM LALLANA (in his programme notes)

75 MILESTONE GOALS

I FEEL FINE

SALAH'S 150TH 19.02.22 V NORWICH

When a team scores as many goals as Liverpool do, it's almost inevitable that some individuals will hit landmark numbers. In recent seasons, Mo Salah and Sadio Mane seem to have hit goal milestones with glorious regularity. It took Salah just over three years to reach 100 goals for the club, hitting his century in the 2-2 draw at Goodison Park in October 2020, though the game was somewhat overshadowed by controversy and a serious injury sustained by Virgil van Dijk. His 100th Premier League goal was also almost forgotten as it arrived in a game at Leeds that Liverpool won, but in which Harvey Elliott received a sickening ankle injury. Such is the rate at which the Egyptian scores, he has already reached 150 for the club in all competitions, doing so in a 3-1 win against Norwich in February 2022, the game that saw Luis Diaz score his first for the club. Sadio Mane reached a couple of milestones in the 2021/22 season, netting his 100th Liverpool goal in the 3-0 win against Crystal Palace in September before notching his 100th Premier League goal in a 5-0 win at Watford the following month. Roberto Firmino also completed his century when he netted his 99th and 100th goals in the 9-0 win against Bournemouth at Anfield in August 2022. It is the first time three Liverpool players have all scored 100 goals under one manager.

MANE'S 100TH 18.09.21 V PALACE

SALAH'S 100TH 17.10.20 V EVERTON

CLOSE TO SIR ROGER

MO SALAH IS THE SECOND-FASTEST LIVERPOOL PLAYER TO REACH 150 GOALS FOR THE CLUB IN ALL COMPETITIONS. HE MANAGED THE TALLY IN JUST 233 MATCHES. ONLY ROGER HUNT (226) REACHED THE MILESTONE IN FEWER GAMES

FIRMINO'S 100TH 27.08.22 V BOURNEMOUTH

I FEEL FINE

A THING OF BEAUTY

Very occasionally a goal is scored at a match that causes an audible murmuring long after the initial roars of celebration have died down with Kopites excitedly talking to each other to try to make sense of what they've just seen. Thiago Alcantara's stunning strike against Porto in the Champions League group stage match at Anfield in November 2021 was one such example. Thiago struck the ball so sweetly from nearly 30 yards out that it hovered about half a metre off the ground for its entire journey from boot to the back of the net, eventually nestling right in the corner. This was the penultimate game of a group stage the Reds had already qualified from, but the lack of jeopardy didn't take anything away from the magnificence of the strike as over 50,000 Reds were just grateful to have witnessed something so beautiful. Mo Salah's goal wrapped up a 2-0 win while Luis Diaz was able to experience an Anfield European night in the flesh just a few months before switching to Merseyside. Thiago's strike was later named UEFA Champions League goal of the season.

I FEEL FINE

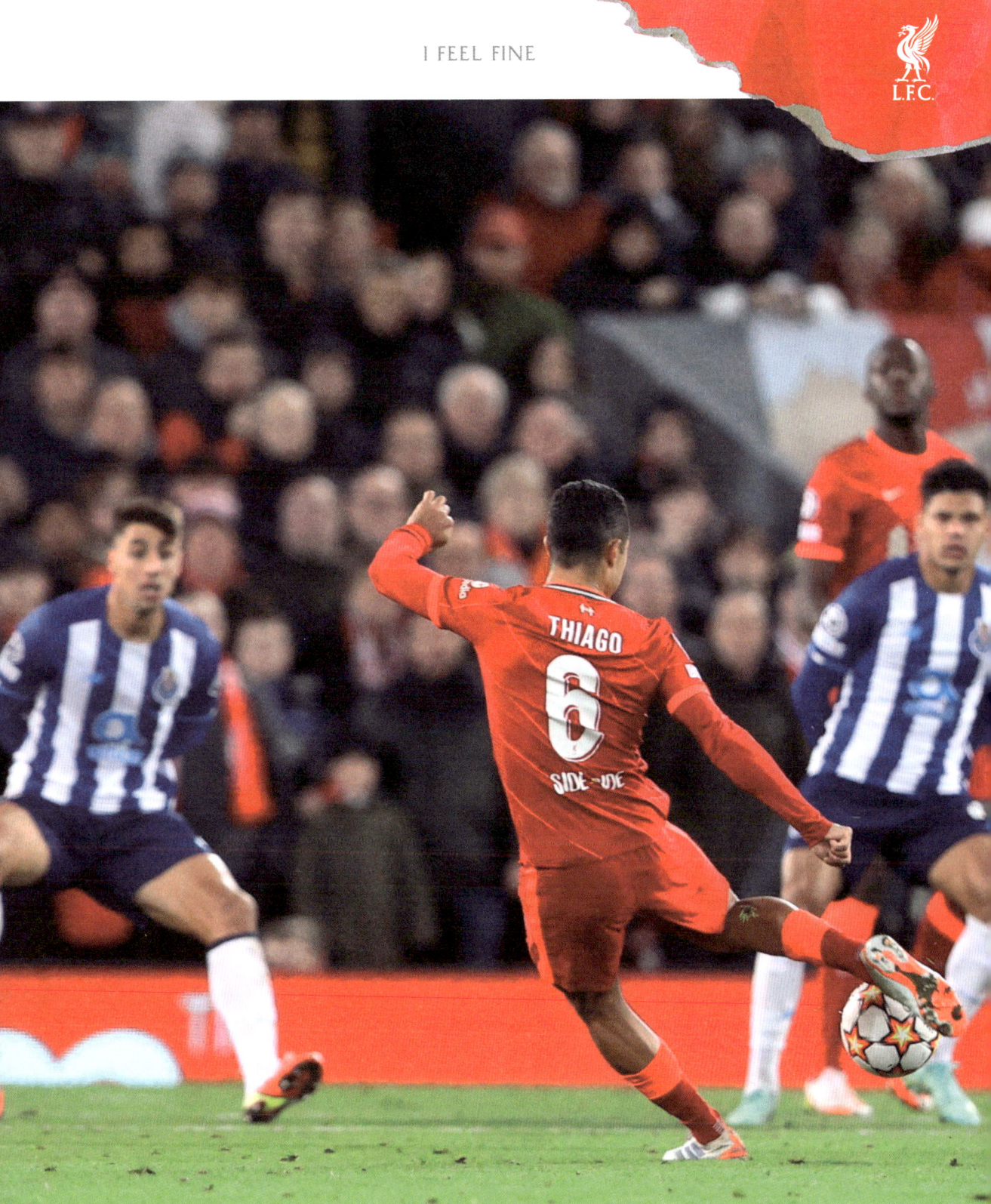

I FEEL FINE

SATURDAY
AND I LIKE THE WAY

West Brom, Everton, Barcelona, Newcastle, Spurs and Arsenal had all been on the receiving end of late, result-changing goals from the GOAT. In December 2021, Wolverhampton Wanderers joined them. With 94 minutes on the clock it looked like two points had been dropped at Molineux, but it was Saturday night and I like the way you move, Divock Origi. Mo Salah cut into the box and played a pass into Origi, who pirouetted like a ballerina in a music box before bludgeoning a low shot past Jose Sa to put the Reds top of the Premier League and add to his already-assured cult-hero status. "If you are not a starter for Liverpool it does not mean you are not a world-class player," said Jürgen Klopp afterwards. "I know some people see it differently from time to time, but in specific moments, Div is outstanding. He had brilliant games for us from the start. In one of the biggest games in our history – against Barcelona, for example – he started, played an incredible game and scored the goals in the right moments. It's just part of his skillset. Divock Origi, the legend, came on and finished it off for us. I love it."

I FEEL FINE

NIGHT YOU MOVE

ADDED-TIME WINNER

SAN SIRO

You wait 13 years to see Liverpool get a win at the San Siro and then two come along at once. The Reds hadn't visited Milan's cathedral of football since playing Internazionale in 2008, but when the 2021/22 Champions League group stage draw was made, a first visit to play AC Milan in Stadio Giuseppe Meazza was on the cards. Incredibly, despite meeting in two Champions League finals and winning 13 European Cups between them, Liverpool and AC Milan had never played each other at Anfield or the San Siro. After beating Milan 3-2 at Anfield on matchday 1, the Reds flew to Lombardy for matchday 6 and recorded a 2-1 victory. Mo Salah equalised Milan's opening goal before Divock Origi headed a historic winner. Incredibly, Liverpool's next Champions League fixture was also in the San Siro after a redraw for the last 16 – a technical error meant the initial draw that placed the Reds with Salzburg was scrapped – paired them with Inter Milan. Jürgen Klopp and his players headed back to the San Siro and won 2-0, Roberto Firmino and Salah getting on the scoresheet. That victory completed the rare double of beating both AC Milan and Inter Milan at the San Siro during the same season, a feat that few Italian clubs have achieved in Serie A.

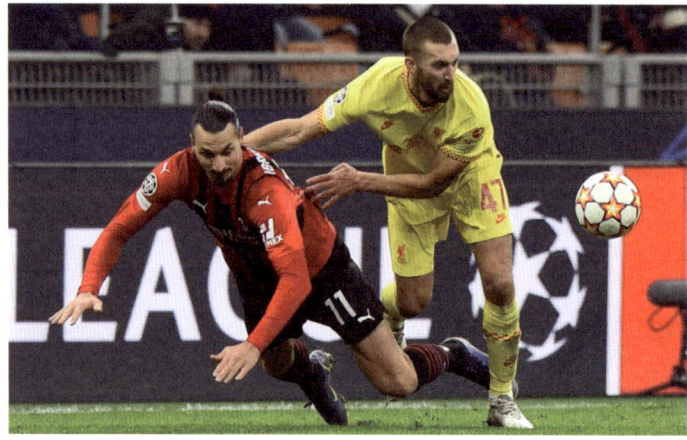

79
WINGMEN

They had their own LFCTV series called 'Wingmen' and while they are primarily defenders, there is no question that Trent Alexander-Arnold and Andy Robertson have reinvented the full-back role under Jürgen Klopp's management. When it comes to assists, their numbers are off the scale. Alexander-Arnold (61) and Robertson (52) kicked off season 2022/23 with an incredible 113 assists between them – an astonishing number for a pair of full-backs. Both set new personal records during the 2021/22 campaign with Alexander-Arnold creating 18 goals and Robertson assisting 15. To give Trent's contribution some context, 18 assists is the same tally that Kevin Keegan (1976/77), Kenny Dalglish (1982/83) and John Barnes (1987/88) made in three of Liverpool's most glorious seasons…and they were all forwards. It's also worth noting that the most assists Steven Gerrard ever got in a season was 16, doing so three times in 2003/04, 2005/06 and 2007/08, although Stevie G did play at full-back at times. While assists have so far only been fully calculated by website lfchistory.net for every season since 1969/70, it could yet be that both Robertson and Alexander-Arnold join an illustrious club in the years to come. Only two Liverpool players have created 20+ goals in a single season for the Reds – Steve McManaman (20) in 1995/96 and the creator supreme Kenny Dalglish, who assisted 21 goals in 1981/82, 23 goals in 1980/81 and a club-record 24 goals in 1984/85. Given Sir Kenny also racked up 19 assists in 1978/79 and in 1979/80, it adds further perspective to both how good he was and how immense the contribution of Alexander-Arnold and Robertson has been to get anywhere close to Dalglish despite playing at full-back. Or are they wingmen?

I FEEL FINE

Most Liverpool FC assists
(from 1969/70 to 2021/22 via lfchistory.net)

	Name	Appearances	Assists
1	Kenny Dalglish	515	167
2	Steven Gerrard	710	145
3	John Barnes	407	101
4	Steve McManaman	364	85
5	Ian Rush	660	83
6	Kevin Keegan	323	72
7	Roberto Firmino	327	67
8	Steve Heighway	475	66
9	Trent Alexander-Arnold	226	61
10	Mo Salah	254	58
11	Terry McDermott	329	57
12	Ray Kennedy	393	55
13	Jordan Henderson	449	55
14	John Toshack	247	54
15	Andy Robertson	224	52

DIOGO JOTA

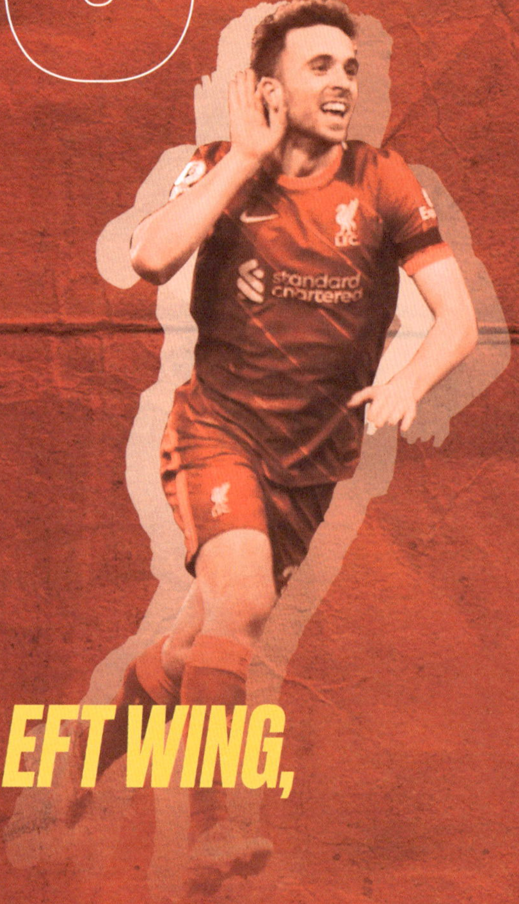

**OHHHHHH,
HE WEARS THE
NUMBER 20,
HE WILL TAKE US
TO VICTORY,
AND WHEN HE'S
RUNNING DOWN THE LEFT WING,
HE'LL CUT INSIDE
AND SCORE FOR LFC.
HE'S A LAD FROM PORTUGAL,
BETTER THAN FIGO DON'T YOU KNOW,
OHHHHH, HIS NAME IS DIO-GO.**

I FEEL FINE

KLOPP PLAYER SONGS XI

During Jürgen Klopp's time as Liverpool manager there have been some brilliant songs for the players. ABBA, James, Whigfield, Creedence Clearwater Revival, Ewan MacColl, the Gibson Brothers and Kungs v Cookin' On Three Burners are among the artists to have inspired these Kop chants. There have been so many that you could pick a Klopp Player Songs XI, so we have. And we're going with a 4-2-3-1 formation (two players here and nine on the next two pages), plus eight subs…

TRENT ALEXANDER-ARNOLD

THE SCOUSER IN OUR TEAM,
THE SCOUSER IN OUR TEAM,
HE'S ALEXANDER-ARNOLD,
HE'S ALEXANDER-ARNOLD,
HE'S ALEXANDER-ARNOLD,
THE SCOUSER IN OUR TEAM.

I FEEL FINE

ALISSON

Alisson! Alisson! Alisson!

ANDY ROBERTSON

*Oh, Andy, Andy,
Andy, Andy, Andy, Andy Robertson!*

VIRGIL VAN DIJK

*He's our centre-half,
He's our number four,
Watch him defend,
And we watch him score.
He'll pass the ball,
Calm as you like,
He's Virgil Van Dijk,
He's Virgil Van Dijk.*

JOE GOMEZ

*Ain't nobody,
Like Joe Gomez,
Makes me happy,
Makes me feel this way.*

THIAGO ALCANTARA

*Thiaaaaago, Thiago Alcantaaaara.
Thiaaaaago, Thiago Alcantaaaara.*

I FEEL FINE

GINI WIJNALDUM

*DER, DER, DER DER DER DER
GINI WIJNALDUM!
DER, DER, DER DER DER DER
GINI WIJNALDUM!*

ROBERTO FIRMINO

*THERE'S SOMETHING THAT
THE KOP WANT YOU TO KNOW,
THE BEST IN THE WORLD
IS BOBBY FIRMINO,
OUR NUMBER NINE,
GIVE HIM THE BALL AND
HE'LL SCORE EVERY TIME,
SÍ SEÑOR,
GIVE THE BALL TO BOBBY
AND HE WILL SCORE.*

SADIO MANE

*SAD-I-O, MANE!
RUNNING DOWN THE WING, MANE!
HERE THE KOPITES SING, MANE!
WHEN WE WON IT IN MADRID.*

MO SALAH

*MO SALAH, MO SALAH, MO SALAH,
RUNNING DOWN THE WING.
SAL-AH-AH-AH-AH-AHHHH,
THE EGYPTIAN KING!*

SUBS:

KOSTAS TSIMIKAS

TSIMI, TSIMI, TSIMI,
OUR KOSTAS TSIMIKAS,
HIS PASSPORT SAYS
HE'S GREEK,
BUT WE ALL KNOW
THAT HE'S SCOUSE

JORDAN HENDERSON

JORDAN, JORDAN HENDERSON,
HENDERSON, HENDERSON, HENDERSON

NABY KEITA

NA-BY KEITA,
NA-BY KEITA,
NA-NA-NA-NA-BY KEITA,
NA-NA-NA-NA-BY KEITA,
BOBBY FIRMINO,
SALAH AND MANE,
(AND ANDY ROBBO!)
NA-BY KEITA, NA-BY KEITA

FABINHO

OLE OLE,
OLE OLE,
FABINHO-O-O, FABINHO-O-O

ALEX OXLADE-CHAMBERLAIN

*YOU TO ME ARE EVERYTHING,
MY ALEX OXLADE-CHAMBERLAIN,
OH BABY, OH BABY*

DIVOCK ORIGI

*SATURDAY NIGHT AND I LIKE
THE WAY YOU MOVE, DIVOCK ORIGI.
HE CUTS INSIDE AND HE SLOTS
IT PAST THE BLUES, DIVOCK ORIGI.
NA NA NA NA NAH, NA NA NA
NA NA NAH, DIVOCK ORIGI.
NA NA NA NA NAH,
NA NA NA NA NA NAH, DIVOCK ORIGI*

TAKUMI MINAMINO

*MINAMINO, HERE WE GO AGAIN,
WHY WHY, SALZBURG EVER LET YOU GO?*

LUIS DIAZ

*OH LUIS DIAZ, OH LUIS DIAZ,
WE SIGNED A LAD FROM FC PORTO,
AND WHEN HE SCORES
HE DANCES WITH DIOGO,
HE PLAYS WITH MANE, SALAH AND FIRMINO,
OH LUIS DIAZ SENDS US ******* LOCO.*

81
ELL OF A JOURNEY

Good things come to those who wait, something Harvey Elliott discovered in February 2022. Four months earlier, the talented teeanger had suffered a serious ankle injury at Leeds United, sidelining him when he was just beginning to make an impression in the Liverpool team. After a successful operation, Harvey patiently worked through his rehabilitation process with Dr Andreas Schlumberger and rehab physio Joe Lewis until the medics and Jürgen Klopp decided he was ready to return as a second-half substitute against Cardiff City in the FA Cup fourth round. Elliott had only been on the pitch for 21 minutes when he flicked up a cross from Andy Robertson and smashed a Kop-end volley into the net to register his first Liverpool goal. "Coming on is already a great step back," said Klopp, "but scoring this nice goal makes it a proper fairytale so I am really happy for him. He was over the moon!" Three weeks later, after making his Champions League debut against Inter Milan in the San Siro, Elliott also came on in the Carabao Cup final against Chelsea and scored Liverpool's ninth penalty when a shoot-out was required to decide the winners. For Harvey Elliott, a comeback from injury, a first Liverpool goal, a Champions League debut and a League Cup winners' medal all arrived in the space of three weeks after four months of rehab. All things come to those who wait.

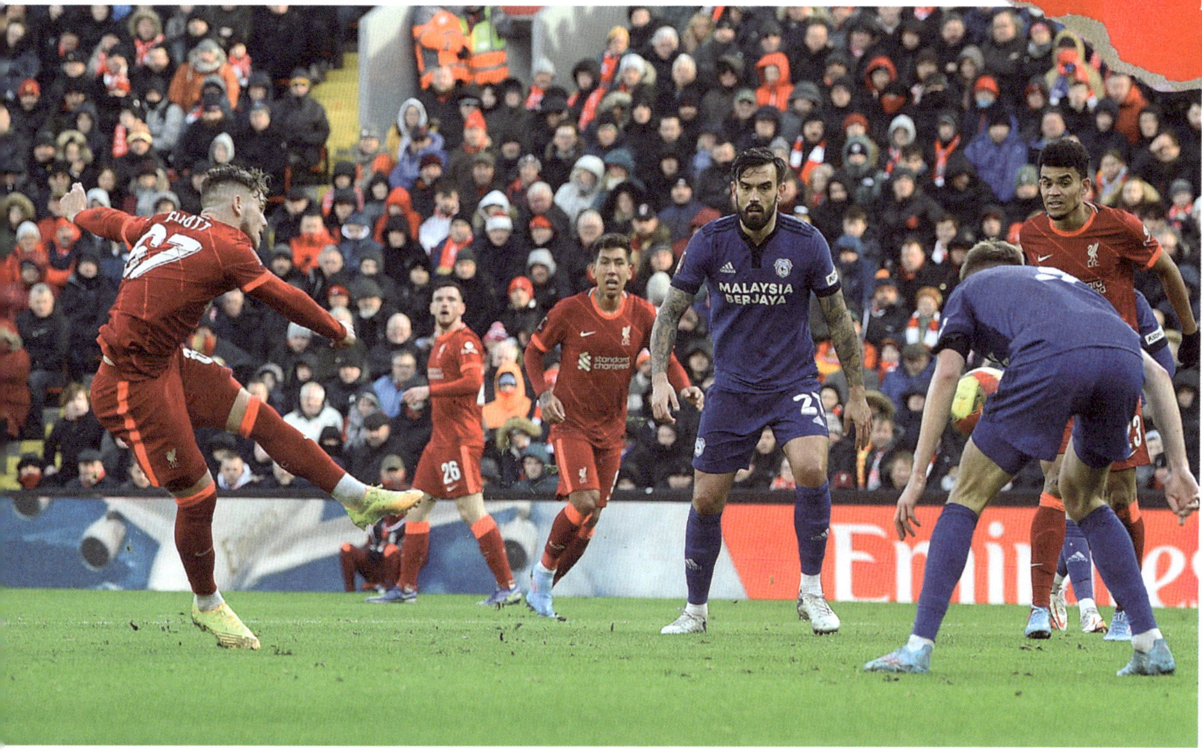
MALAYSIA
BERJAYA

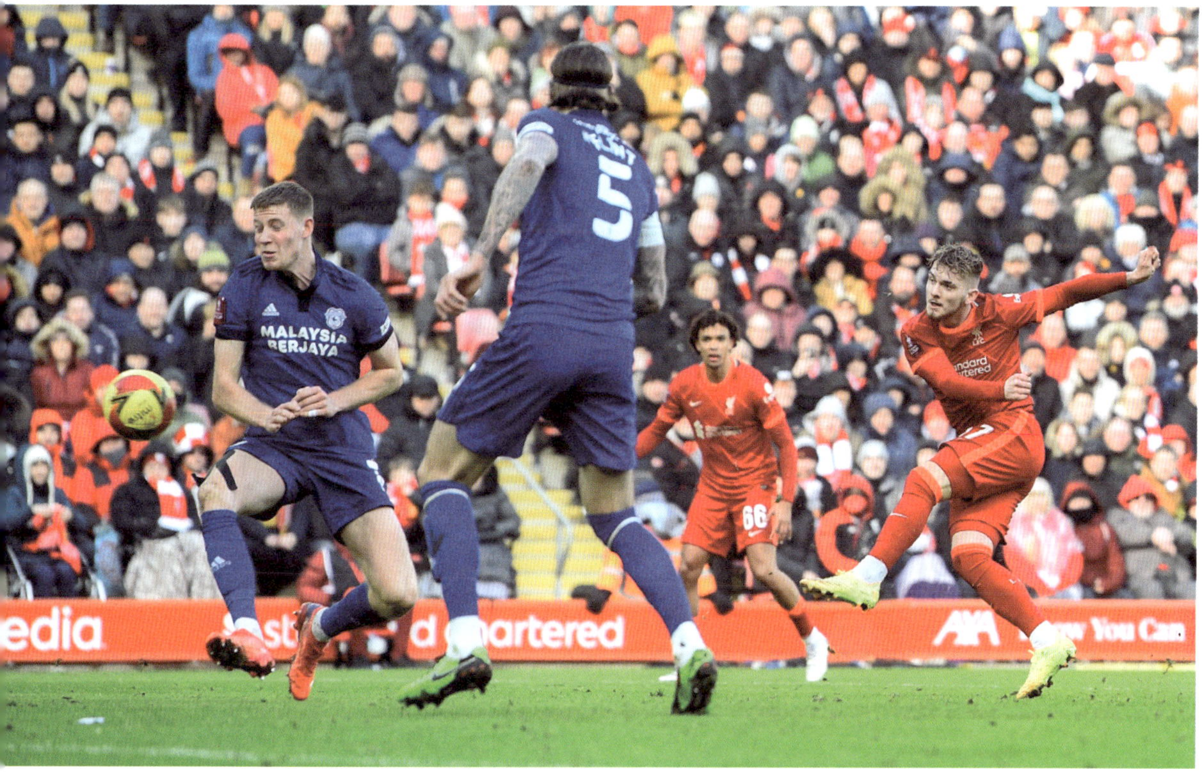
MALAYSIA
BERJAYA

I FEEL FINE

PASS MASTERS

Liverpool have long prided themselves on their 'pass and move' philosophy. You could argue it's a Liverpool groove. Keeping the ball moving in the hope of unsettling opposition defences to create spaces to exploit is not a new idea and there can rarely have been a better example of that passing identity than the sequence of 34 passes that resulted in Luis Diaz scoring against Norwich City in February 2022 for what was his first Liverpool goal. Starting with Jordan Henderson, 10 players touched the ball at least once as they kept possession for over a minute-and-a-half. And it was Henderson who spotted the gap that eventually opened up to release the final pass into the path of Diaz, who lifted the ball beautifully over Angus Gunn to complete the scoring in a 3-1 win. It was Liverpool's 100th goal of the season.

I FEEL FINE

THE 34 PASSES...

Henderson > Van Dijk > Henderson > Van Dijk > Mane > Matip > Gomez > Diaz > Salah > Henderson > Salah > Henderson > Salah > Henderson > Gomez > Thiago > Mane > Van Dijk > Mane > Matip > Gomez > Alisson > Thiago > Tsimikas > Henderson > Thiago > Salah > Thiago > Salah > Thiago > Gomez > Salah > Thiago > Henderson > Diaz

83

I FEEL FINE

FEELING PUMPED

It has become a taken-for-granted part of Liverpool matchdays now. Something that always happens – win, lose or draw. Yet before Jürgen Klopp arrived at Anfield, Liverpool managers coming onto the centre of the pitch at full-time to dish out handshakes was rare. Liverpool managers coming on to give hugs was even rarer. And Liverpool managers running down to the Kop to celebrate victories with three fist pumps? Absolutely unheard of. "I come onto the pitch at the end to thank our supporters," explained the Liverpool boss after bringing a part of German footballing culture to Anfield. "If I could shake the hand of every one of them I would." Being a visible presence on the pitch at full-time, no matter the result, is one of the ways that Klopp quickly bonded with Liverpool supporters. He never hides, but then his teams have been so good that more often than not he heads down to the Kop after a Liverpool win and that often means one thing… three trademark celebratory fist pumps, each cheered with gusto by those in the Anfield stands.

Klopp sometimes shies away from the distinctive gesture when the on-pitch TV camera operators get too close – Jürgen's fist pumps are a shared moment of collective joy, not a 'look at me I'm on TV' action – but then he has also got carried away once or twice. When the Reds beat Leeds United 6-0 at Anfield in February 2022, Klopp celebrated with six fist pumps, one for each goal. And after Liverpool's FA Cup final victory against Chelsea, he took his fist pumps on tour! The Reds boss punched their air with joy 12 times in total with three fist pumps given to travelling Kopites on both sides of Wembley, and three next to either side of the goal at the stadium's West End. It was a numerical upgrade on what happened after the FA Cup semi-final success against Manchester City in north London. Klopp looked set to head down the Wembley tunnel without raising his clenched fist until James Milner had a word in his ear. "Milly told me to do it!" he admitted. "I actually wanted to go [because he was being followed by a camera] but Milly said 'you have to'. So I did it because of Milly. I think in this moment it's really important to say as well, because it was really special and we all felt it was really special, the atmosphere our people created here was second to none." Three cheers to that, Jürgen.

I FEEL FINE

"IF I COULD SHAKE THE HANDS OF EVERY ONE OF THEM, I WOULD"

– JÜRGEN KLOPP

84 LEGENDS

I FEEL FINE

Nothing lasts forever, including the careers of footballers, but when you're an ex-Liverpool FC player it doesn't necessarily mean you'll never play at Anfield again, even when you've retired. In March 2017, Liverpool FC's official charity – the LFC Foundation – hosted the first ever official Legends game at Anfield with Real Madrid Leyendas the esteemed visitors. Steven Gerrard, Robbie Fowler, John Aldridge, Jerzy Dudek and Patrik Berger were among the legends to play and it was Gerrard who struck the winner in a 4-3 victory with ex-Red Fernando Morientes on the scoresheet for Real Madrid. A sell-out Anfield crowd of 54,000 raised over £1,000,000 for the LFC Foundation and it proved to be such a popular event that it was held again in 2018. This time Xabi Alonso and Dirk Kuyt made their Liverpool returns against FC Bayern Legends, who had Lothar Matthaus making his Anfield debut. Alonso played for both sides and thought he'd won it for Bayern Munich with a free-kick only for Bjorn Tore Kvarme to net an unlikely 90th-minute equaliser in an entertaining 5-5 draw. Milan Glorie were the next legends to visit Anfield in 2019 and fielded the likes of Dida, Costacurta, Cafu, Kaka, Rui Costa, Pirlo and Inzaghi, but were on the end of a 3-2 defeat with Gerrard netting the winner. Due to the coronavirus pandemic a two-year break followed until Liverpool Legends made a welcome return against Barca Legends in March 2022. Managed by Sir Kenny Dalglish, Milan Baros and Maxi Rodriguez both made their Legends debuts and Gerrard opened the scoring, but an equaliser followed by a Rivaldo penalty gave the Catalans a 2-1 success to become the first visiting legends team to win at Anfield. Who knows, maybe Jürgen Klopp and his current crop of players will be involved in these feel-good fundraising fixtures in the future.

I FEEL FINE

I FEEL FINE

OUT TO (IM)PRESS

Liverpool's 2-2 draw with Brighton at Anfield in October 2021 isn't one most Kopites care to recall as two precious Premier League points were dropped, but an incident during it inspired a Reds goal at Wembley six months later. As Brighton tried to play out from the back, the Redmen pressed so intensely that when Seagulls keeper Robert Sanchez received the ball near his goalline, Sadio Mane was on top of him. Sanchez's attempted clearance struck Mane as he slid in and the ball ricocheted into the Kop-end net, but a VAR review showed it had deflected off Sadio's foot onto his arm. The goal was chalked off, but even so, Jürgen Klopp described it as: "My favourite goal of all six years in Liverpool because of how we put them under pressure there – it was just insane and unlucky with the handball." Half-a-year later, Mane was leading Liverpool's press in the FA Cup semi-final against Manchester City at Wembley. This time,

I FEEL FINE

"THE FIRST GOAL HE SCORED, *I LOVE IT*. THE ACCELERATION OF SADIO, THE *DESIRE* TO GET THERE, IT WAS REALLY *GREAT*"

– JÜRGEN KLOPP ON MANE

when goalkeeper Zack Steffen hesitated while in possession, Mane sprinted towards him, slid in and the ball flew into the net off his foot. The travelling Kop erupted and it made his manager happy too. "Sadio was the first player to start the press, so it was intense for him as well," he said. "The first goal he scored, I love it. The acceleration of Sadio, the desire to get there, it was really great." You get the impression that impressive pressing impresses the boss.

I FEEL FINE

86

WE ARE ZEN OF JÜRGEN'S BEST

Goals. You've just got to celebrate them. And when you're Mo Salah you've got a lot of goals to celebrate. The Egyptian King doesn't have the same repertoire of celebrations as Roberto Firmino – who has marked goals by whipping off his shirt, dancing with Philippe Coutinho and Sadio Mane, covering an eye, shooting pistols, jumping over advertising hoardings at Arsenal and almost kung-fu kicking his team-mates when they score – but Mo does have a range of yoga-

I FEEL FINE

I FEEL FINE

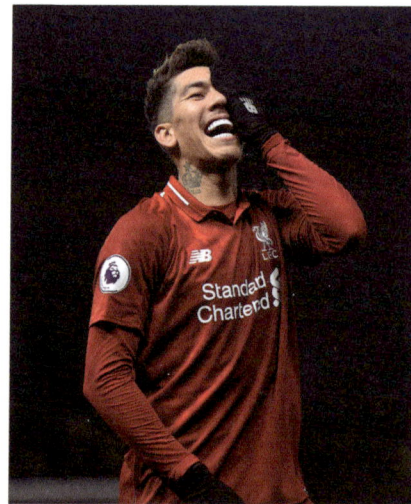

I FEEL FINE

inspired celebrations. After scoring against former club Chelsea at Anfield in 2019, Salah celebrated with a Vrksasana [tree pose] – standing on one leg in front of the Kop, closing his eyes and clasping his hands together as if in prayer. A fortnight later, after netting in a 5-0 win against Huddersfield Town, he sat cross-legged on the Anfield turf in the lotus position, which was quite ironic given the Kop's Salah song is inspired by James' hit Sit Down. Following a three-year hiatus from post-goal yoga – and after Diogo Jota performed his own sit down celebration when pretending to play EA Sports' FIFA22 on a joypad when scoring against Southampton – Salah revived the Vrksasana. He was back on one leg at the Anfield Road end when he struck his first of two goals during the Reds' 4-0 Anfield victory against Manchester United…and followed it up with the same celebration after netting his second. Maybe Mo should be wearing the number zen shirt…

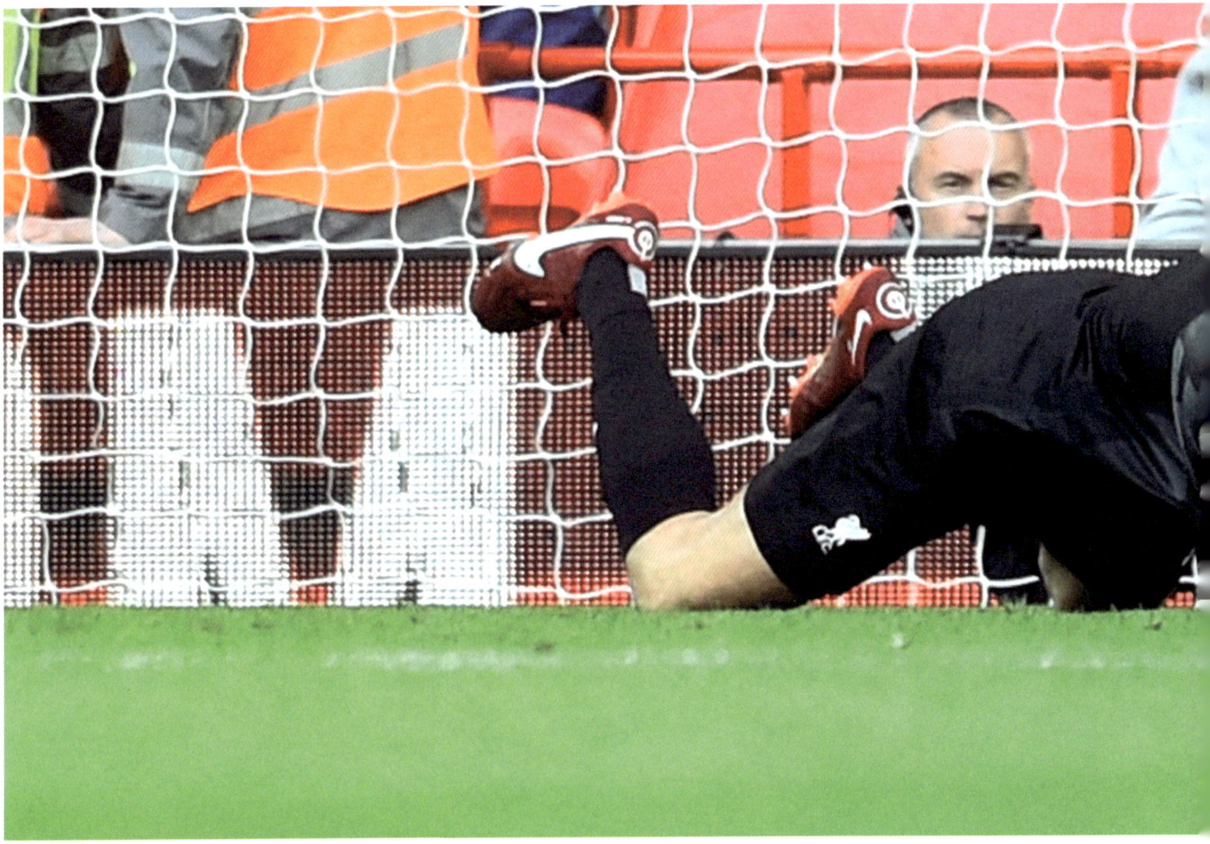

POLICE
HEAD STEWARD
HEAD STEWARD
23
A.BECKER

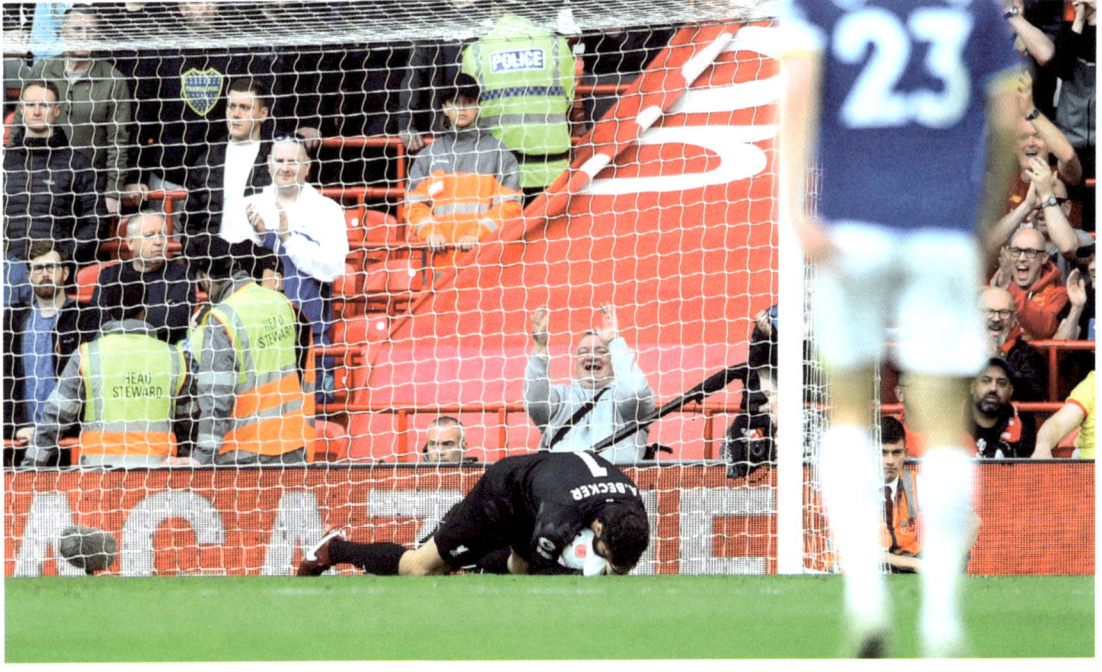

I FEEL FINE

ALI GENIUS

Kopites got used to having a goalkeeper with a sense of humour when Bruce Grobbelaar was Liverpool's number one in the 1980s. From swinging on the crossbar, doing handstands and covering opponents' eyes to throwing snowballs at assistant referees and balancing umbrellas on his nose, Grobbelaar made Liverpool supporters laugh. In April 2022, Alisson Becker showed Anfield that he has a sense of humour too. During the opening hour of the 240th Merseyside derby, Everton slowed the game down at every conceivable opportunity. "Jordan Pickford deliberated over his goal-kicks as if he was choosing a mortgage," wrote Jonathan Liew in The Guardian with one tactic deployed by the Everton goalkeeper being to unnecessarily dive onto the turf when collecting the ball. Eventually the Reds broke the Blues down, scoring through Andy Robertson and Divock Origi to win 2-0, and shortly before full-time Alisson sent Anfield into raptures of laughter when he easily gathered a shot from Richarlison before plunging to the turf, mimicking his opponent's earlier behaviour. It was a hilarious end to an afternoon when Liverpool stretched the gap between the two clubs to 50 points in the Premier League table, the biggest ever on the day of a Merseyside derby.

ULLA WANTS TO STAY

Building a successful football club isn't just about hiring the right manager or signing the right players, it's about keeping hold of them too. So when news emerged in April 2022 that Jürgen Klopp had shelved his plan to return to Germany in 2024 and had instead signed a deal that would extend his stay as Liverpool boss until 2026, it felt like the Reds had just won another cup final. "Ulla wants to stay and as a good husband what are you doing when your wife wants to stay? You are staying," he said. "The most important contract in my life is the one with Ulla. That's where it started again. We sat in the kitchen at the table and Ulla said, 'I can't see us leaving in 2024'. And I was like, 'What?!' 'No, really, [with] all the people about...' When I thought about it then it was clear I needed to have one more really important conversation and that was with Pep Lijnders. He is probably the main reason for it because he is a real energiser – this man is on fire and our connection is beyond football things. When he said, 'Oh, yes, I am in!' then it was clear that we are open for any kind of talks." With Klopp's Anfield stay extended it gave the players added clarity about the future and in the summer of 2022, Mo Salah also signed a new long-term contract. "It takes a little bit of time, I think, to renew, but now everything is done so we just need to focus on what's next," said the Egyptian King. "We are in a good position to fight for everything. We just need to keep working hard, have a good vision, be positive and go for everything again." The Liverpool manager is staying until 2026 and with many key members of his squad having also committed their futures to LFC to between 2025 and 2027, it isn't just Ulla Klopp who wanted to stay on Merseyside for the foreseeable future.

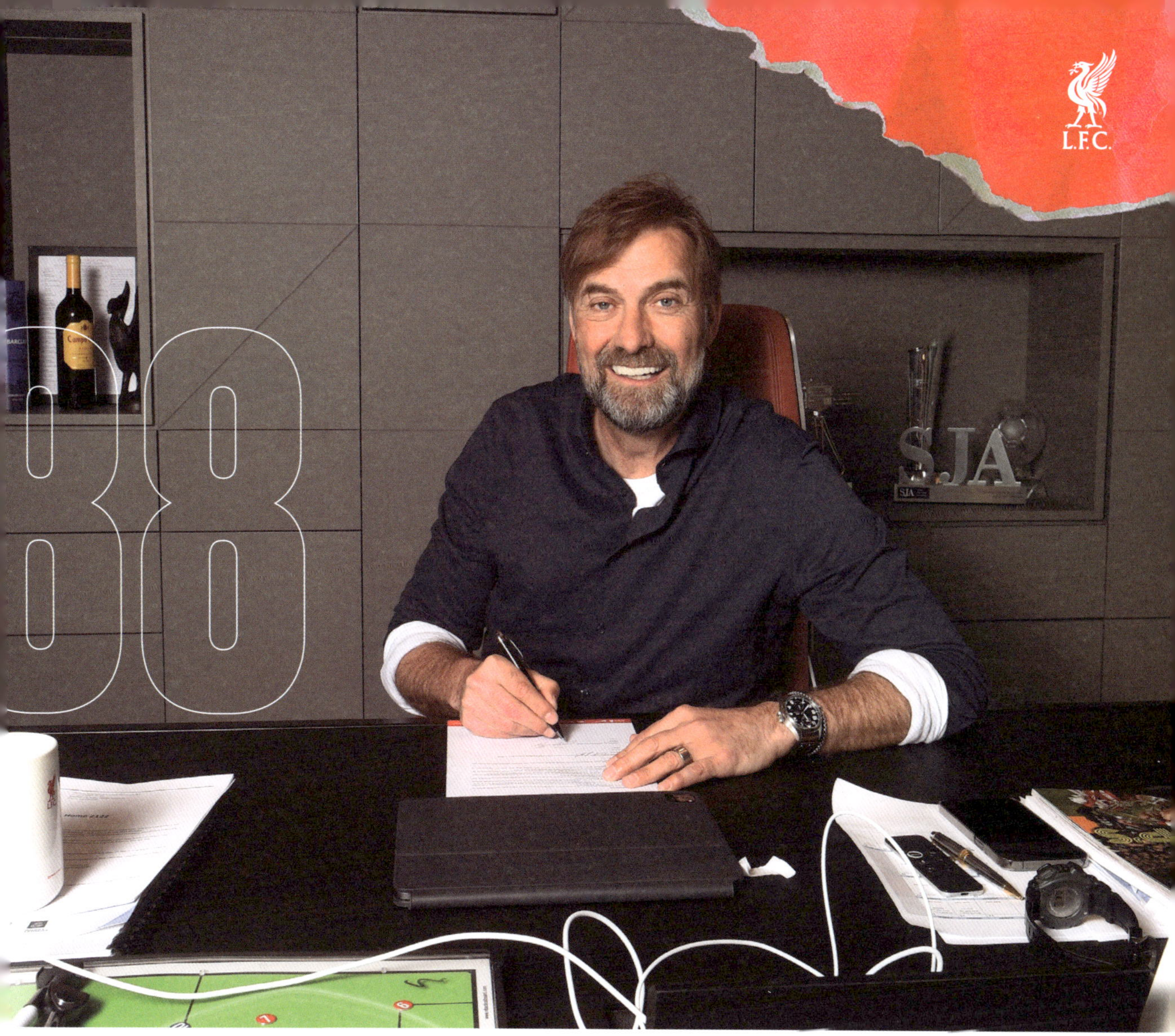
38
L.F.C.
SJA

AXA

AXA
LFCTV GO
standard chartered
Expedia
67

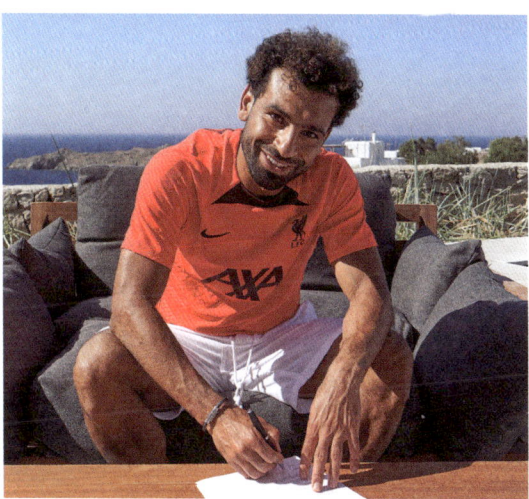

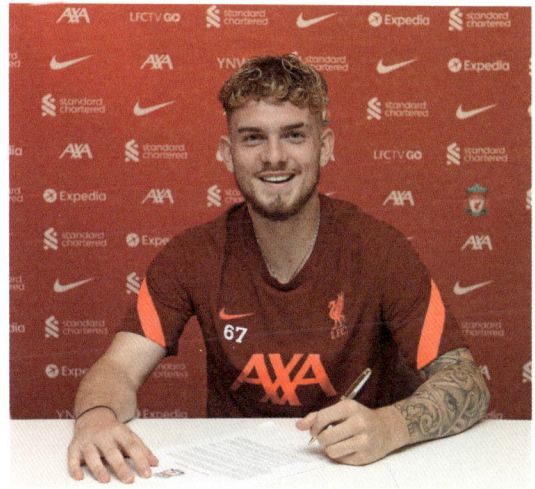

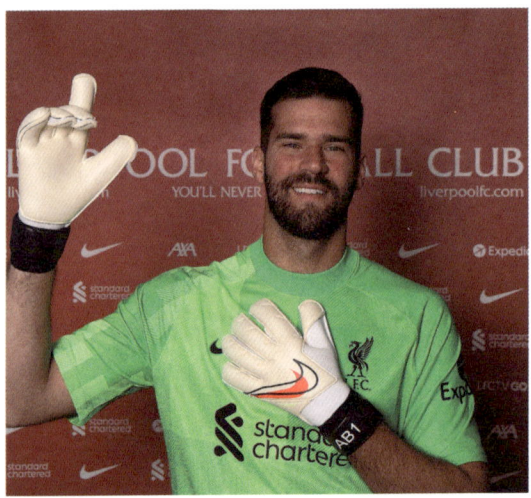

"TO CONTINUE THIS JOURNEY IS INCREDIBLE FOR ME AND MY FAMILY, AND I HOPE THE FANS AND THE CLUB FEEL THE SAME WAY"
– JORDAN HENDERSON, AUGUST 2021

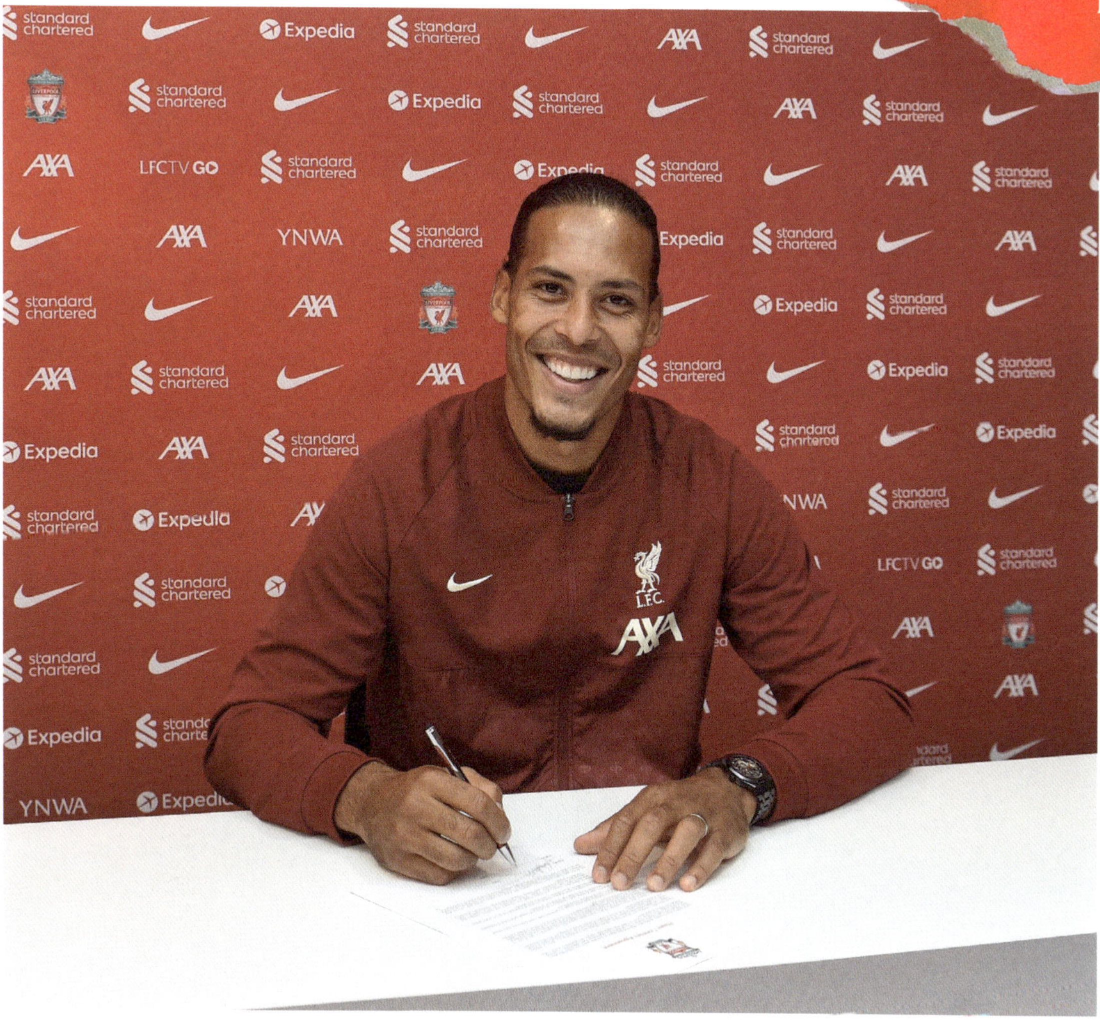
standard chartered
Expedia
AXA
LFCTV GO
YNWA
L.F.C.

standard chartered
Expedia
AXA
YNWA
LFCTV GO

AXA
LFCTV GO
standard chartered
Expedia
YNWA
47

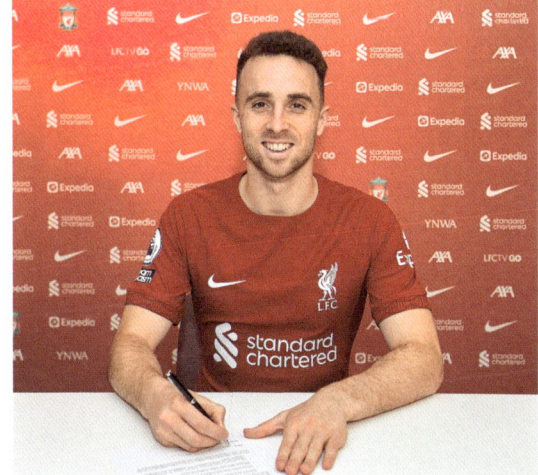

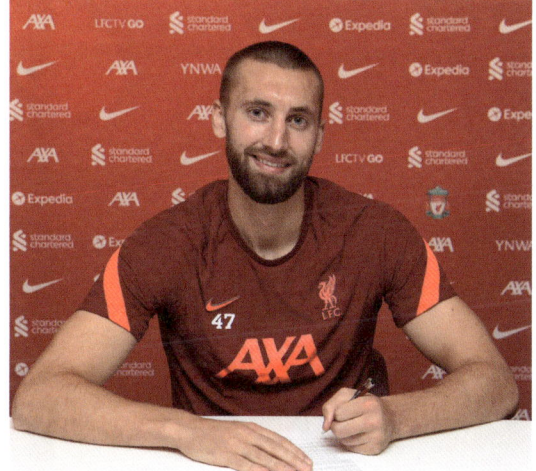

SOME PEOPLE ARE ON THE PITCH...

89

It's not a phenomenon that is unique to Liverpool FC, but the annual lap of honour is one of the more wholesome Anfield experiences. Apart from a break due to COVID-19, the last home game of the season has been an opportunity for fans, players and staff to demonstrate their mutual appreciation. After that day's match is finished, the players briefly return to the dressing room, only to re-emerge to roars from an expectant crowd. And it isn't just the players that star in these particular shows. Their partners and children come out to say hello too, with the kids, in particular, relishing their chance to kick a ball around on the hallowed turf and even put it in the back of the Kop end goal...yes, we know who Mo Salah's daughter takes after in that regard! Kopites also take the opportunity to hand over their own awards (the Golden Sambas) to the Red All Over The Land player and young player of the year. And in recent years the occasion has sometimes been used to wish the team well before they headed off to a final European engagement of the season. All together now: 'Just like the team that's gonna win the European Cup (again!), we shall not be moved...'

GOODBYES TO GOOD BUYS

Not every Liverpool FC player gets the Anfield farewell they deserve at the end of their final season for the club. Often it can be unclear if a player is staying or moving on when the final home game comes around, but when Kopites know a loyal servant is destined for pastures new they aren't shy of showing their appreciation. Lucas Leiva received rapturous applause when coming on to make his final Anfield appearance against Middlesbrough in 2017. The Brazilian, who spent a decade on Merseyside, was also presented with a gold '21' trophy in recognition of his squad number and made an on-pitch speech. "It's been an incredible 10 years," he said. "We all know it's been a little bit like a rollercoaster, a lot of ups and downs, but I'm so proud to wear this shirt every day of my life." Adam Lallana and Dejan Lovren were denied Anfield send-offs after Liverpool's 2020 Premier League title win due to the coronavirus pandemic closing the turnstiles, but at least Gini Wijnaldum had the applause of 10,000 Reds ringing in his ears when given a guard of honour by his team-mates ahead of his departure in 2021. Wijnaldum was presented with a framed Champions Wall by LFC CEO Billy Hogan and a year later Divock Origi received an updated version of it when he too was given a guard of honour at a full Anfield following the final home game of the 2021/22 campaign. Jürgen Klopp described the Belgian as "one of the most important players I ever had," but it was a legendary Kop banner that truly said 'ta ra' to the ultimate Liverpool cult hero: FOOTBALL WITHOUT ORIGI IS NOTHING.

I FEEL FINE

91

LIVING THE DREAM

Major trophy number 49 in the club's history is memorable for lots of reasons. The Reds faced Chelsea in the final of the Carabao Cup in February 2022 at a time when Liverpool were still fighting on all four fronts. Jürgen Klopp decided to stick with Caoimhin Kelleher in goal, the Irishman having done so well in the earlier rounds. Plans hit a major snag pre-match as Thiago Alcantara was injured in the warm-up. The game itself was as entertaining as it gets for a 0-0. Disallowed goals, big chances, woodwork struck – and then the ultimate drama...a penalty shoot-out. But it was no ordinary shoot-out. Chelsea brought on their penalty-saving specialist keeper, Kepa

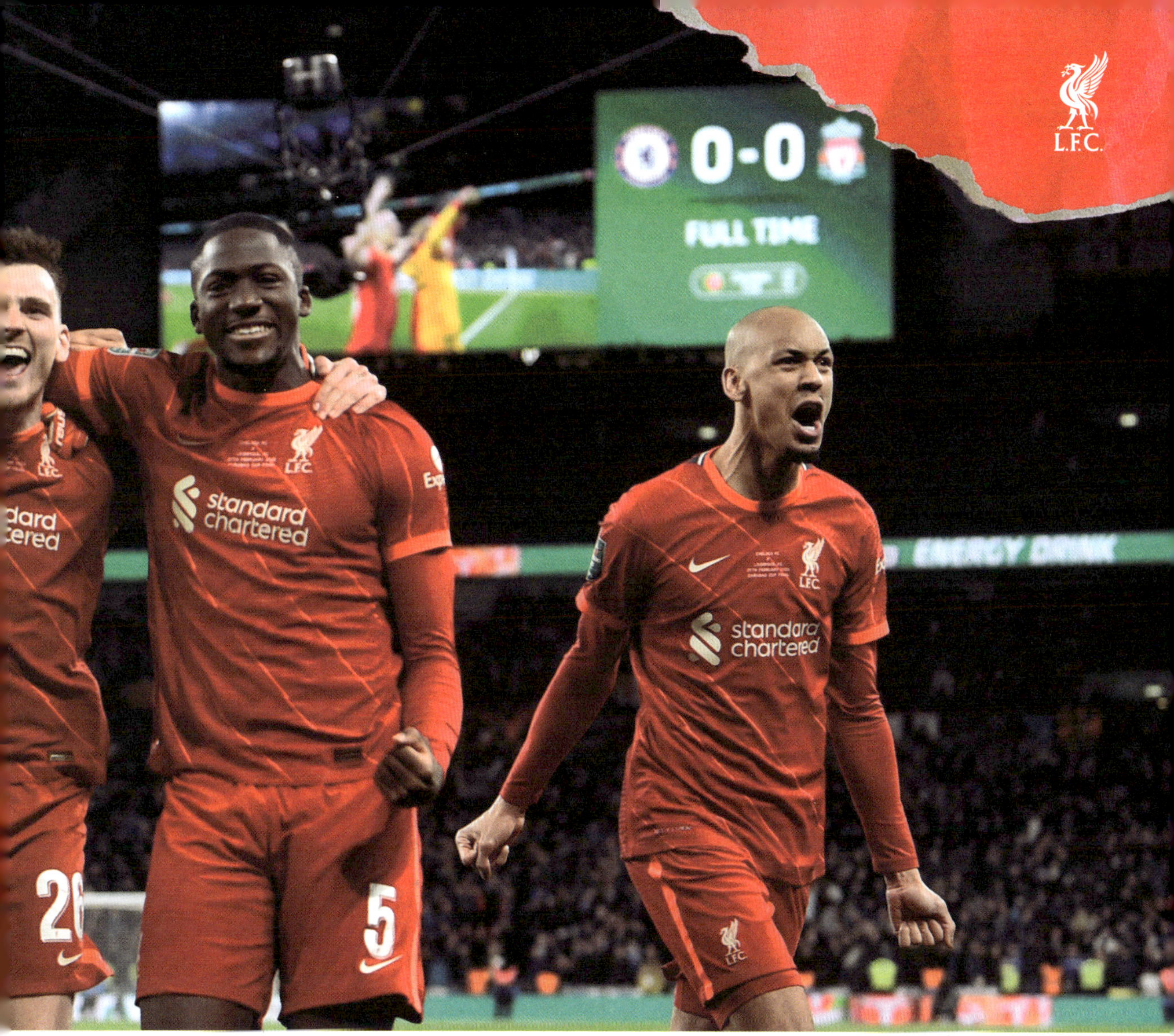
0-0
FULL TIME
standard chartered
standard chartered
ENERGY DRINK

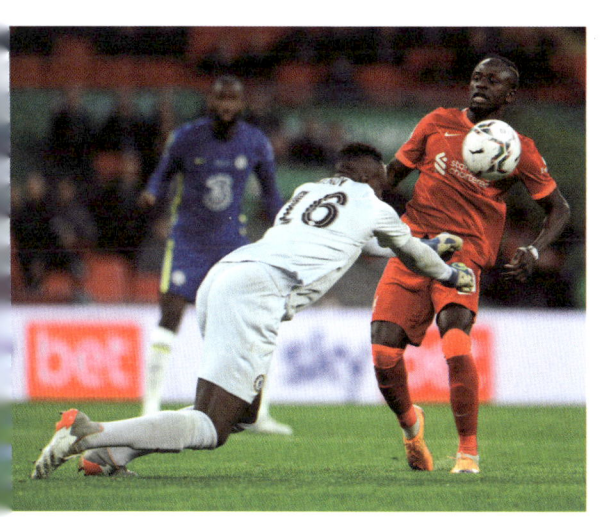

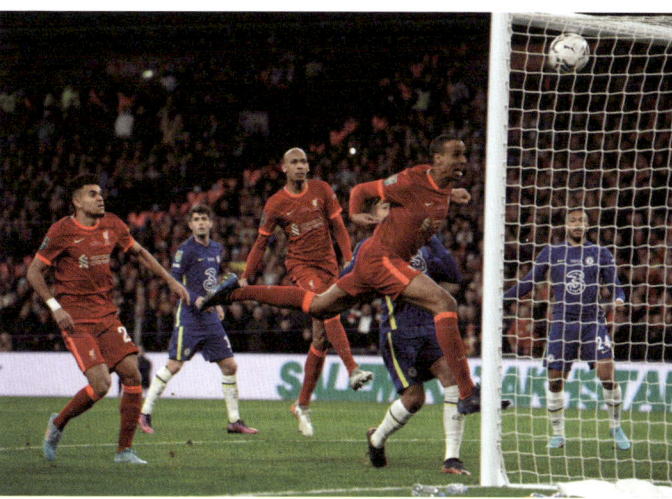

Arrizabalaga, but after every outfield player had taken a penalty it was 10-10. Over to the keepers. Kelleher stepped up and emphatically rammed the ball home, admitting afterwards that he changed his mind what to do during the run-up. Arrizabalaga was nowhere near as composed, blasting his effort well over the bar. The players went wild; the travelling Kop went wild; Liverpool had won League Cup number nine. One more and the Reds would have a half-century of major trophies...and we didn't have long to wait.

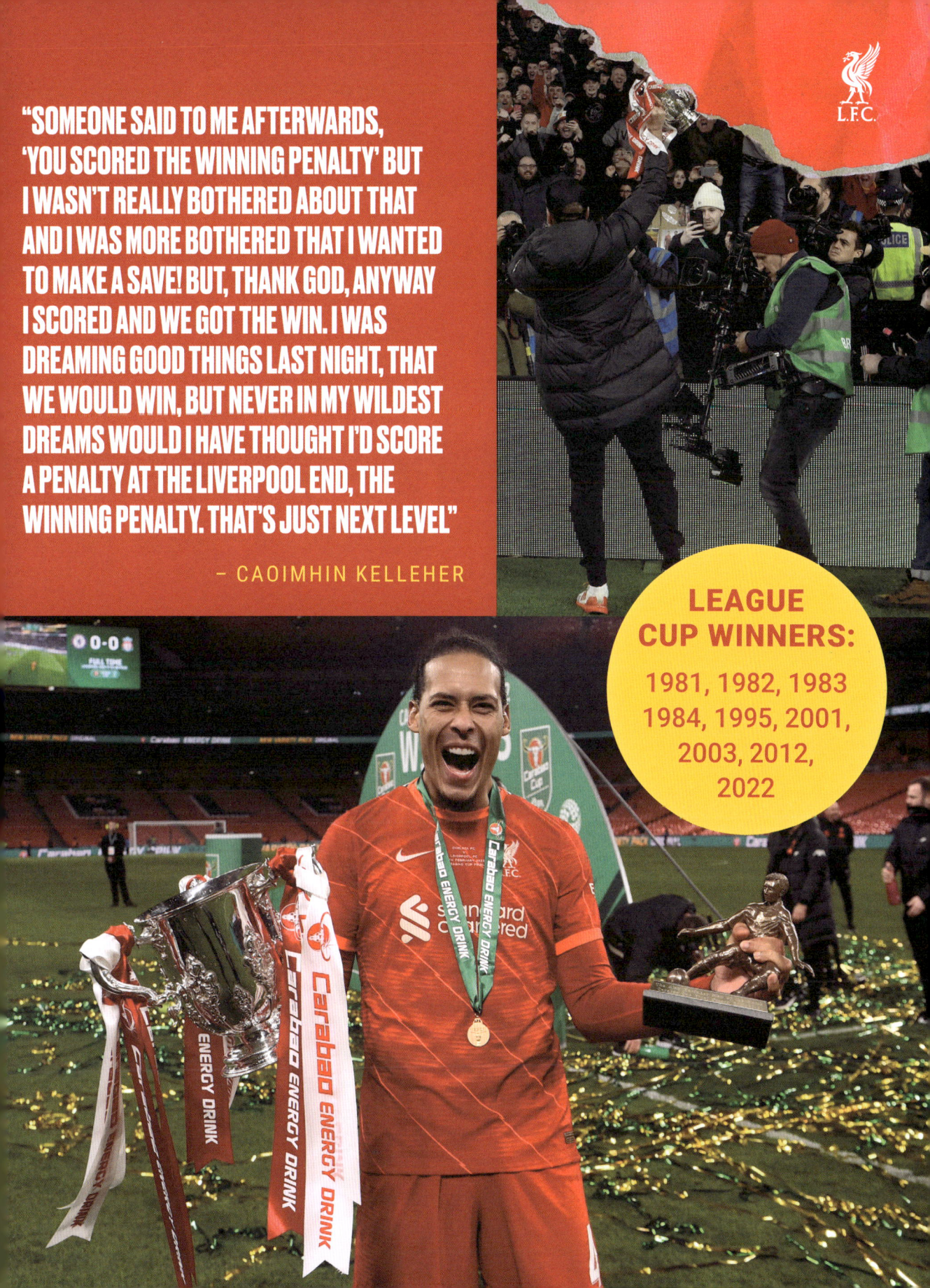

"SOMEONE SAID TO ME AFTERWARDS, 'YOU SCORED THE WINNING PENALTY' BUT I WASN'T REALLY BOTHERED ABOUT THAT AND I WAS MORE BOTHERED THAT I WANTED TO MAKE A SAVE! BUT, THANK GOD, ANYWAY I SCORED AND WE GOT THE WIN. I WAS DREAMING GOOD THINGS LAST NIGHT, THAT WE WOULD WIN, BUT NEVER IN MY WILDEST DREAMS WOULD I HAVE THOUGHT I'D SCORE A PENALTY AT THE LIVERPOOL END, THE WINNING PENALTY. THAT'S JUST NEXT LEVEL"

– CAOIMHIN KELLEHER

LEAGUE CUP WINNERS:
1981, 1982, 1983, 1984, 1995, 2001, 2003, 2012, 2022

"THE GAME HE [KELLEHER] PLAYED TONIGHT WAS ABSOLUTELY INCREDIBLE. I'M NOT 100 PER CENT SURE I HAVE THE FULL STORY OF THE WHOLE GAME BUT I CAN REMEMBER AT LEAST TWO INCREDIBLE SAVES – PROBABLY THERE WERE MORE. SO, HE PROVED THAT THE DECISION TO LINE HIM UP WAS ABSOLUTELY RIGHT. AND THEN IN A VERY SPECTACULAR PENALTY SHOOT-OUT, HE SHOWED THE WHOLE RANGE OF HIS SKILLSET. FIRST AND FOREMOST, HE'S A GOALKEEPER BUT HE FINISHED ONE OFF WITH HIS REALLY SKILLED FEET. TOP-CLASS"

— JÜRGEN KLOPP

Chelsea's penalty takers:
Marcos Alonso
Romelu Lukaku
Kai Havertz
Reece James
Jorginho
Antonio Rudiger
N'Golo Kante
Timo Werner
Thiago Silva
Trevoh Chalobah
Kepa Arrizabalaga

Liverpool's penalty takers:
James Milner
Fabinho
Virgil van Dijk
Trent Alexander-Arnold
Mo Salah
Diogo Jota
Divock Origi
Andy Robertson
Harvey Elliott
Ibrahima Konate
Caoimhin Kelleher

FANTASTIC FIFTY

The similarities between the Carabao Cup final and the FA Cup final were remarkable. The same opponents. The same venue. The same scoreline. The same penalty shoot-out decider. And what some might see as an unlikely matchwinner. Liverpool were facing Chelsea again, nearly three months after their previous final meeting. This was a tighter affair than the League Cup final with the drama initially provided by injury scares to Mo Salah and Virgil van Dijk, who both left the field with big games in the Premier League and Champions League still to play. So a penalty shoot-out was needed again. And again, the score was level after five spot-kicks each and went to sudden death. Eventually Mason Mount had his effort saved by Alisson, and our Greek Scouser, Kostas Tsimikas, stepped forward to strike into the bottom left-hand corner before embarking on a wild, curved run and being mobbed by his team-mates. Jordan Henderson was getting back ache from lifting so many trophies and the Reds had won the 50th major honour in the club's history.

I FEEL FINE

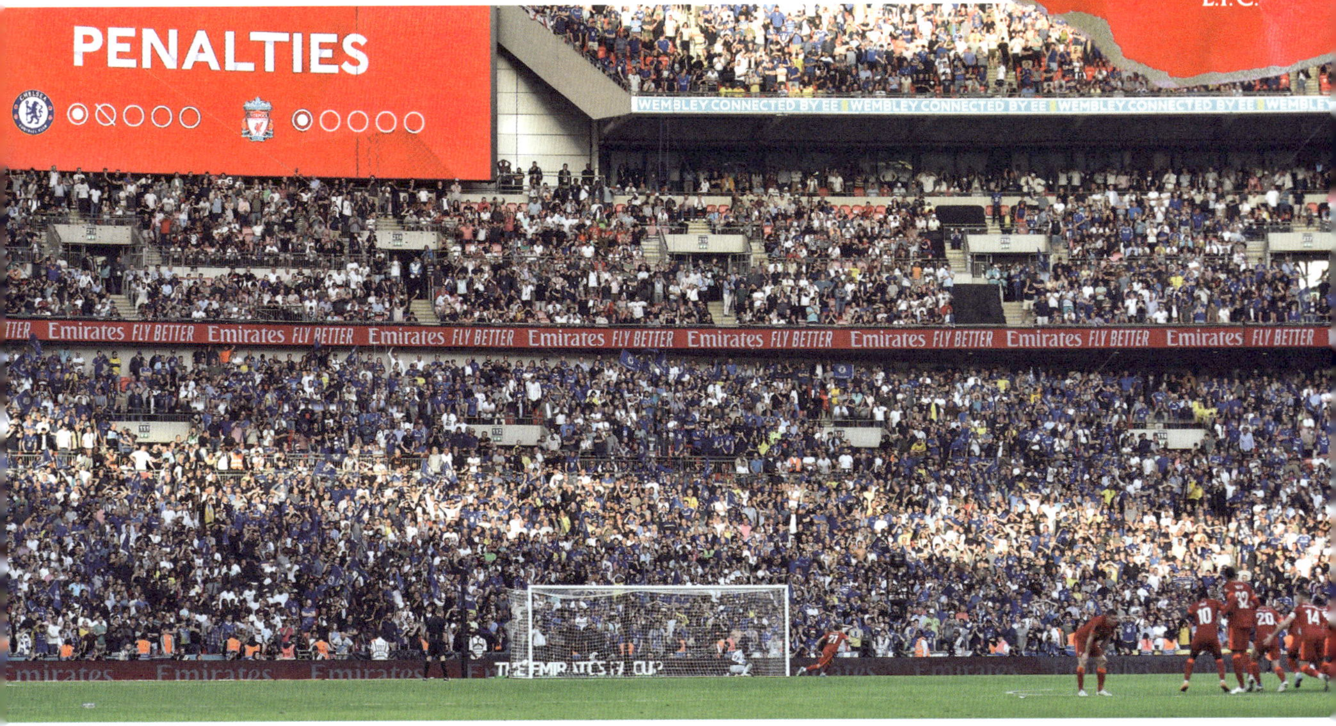
PENALTIES
WEMBLEY CONNECTED BY EE
Emirates FLY BETTER
THE EMIRATES FA CUP

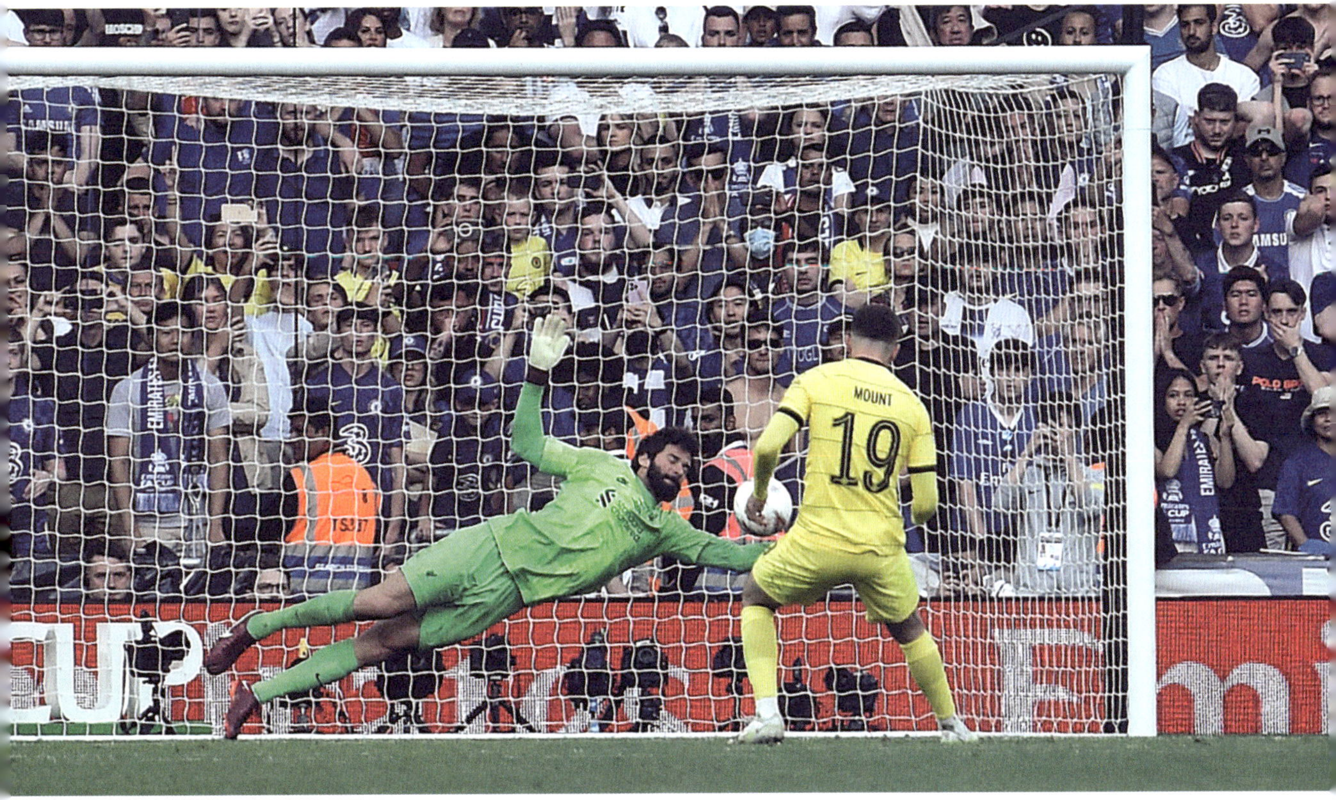
MOUNT
19

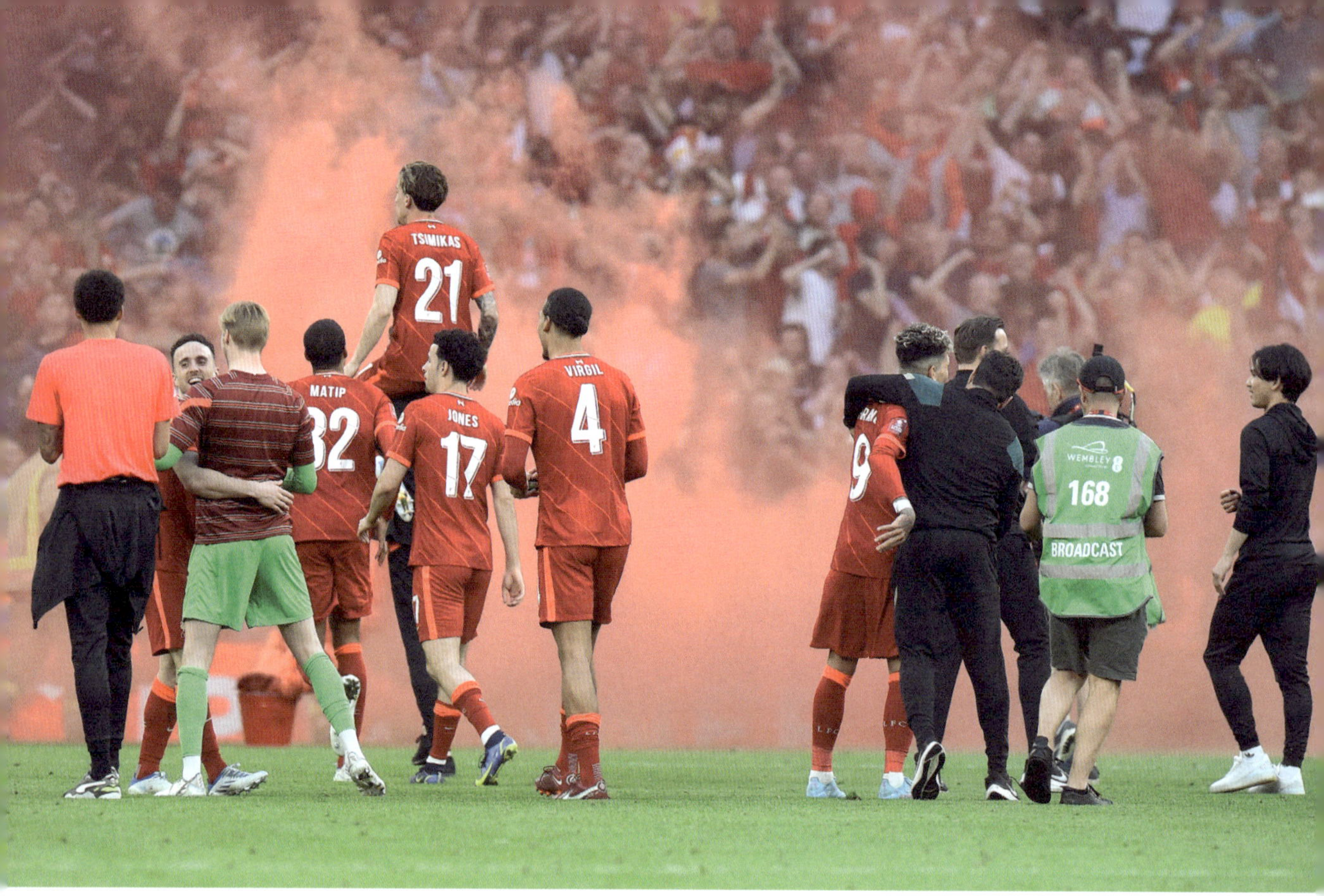
TSIMIKAS
21
MATIP
32
JONES
17
VIRGIL
4
168
BROADCAST

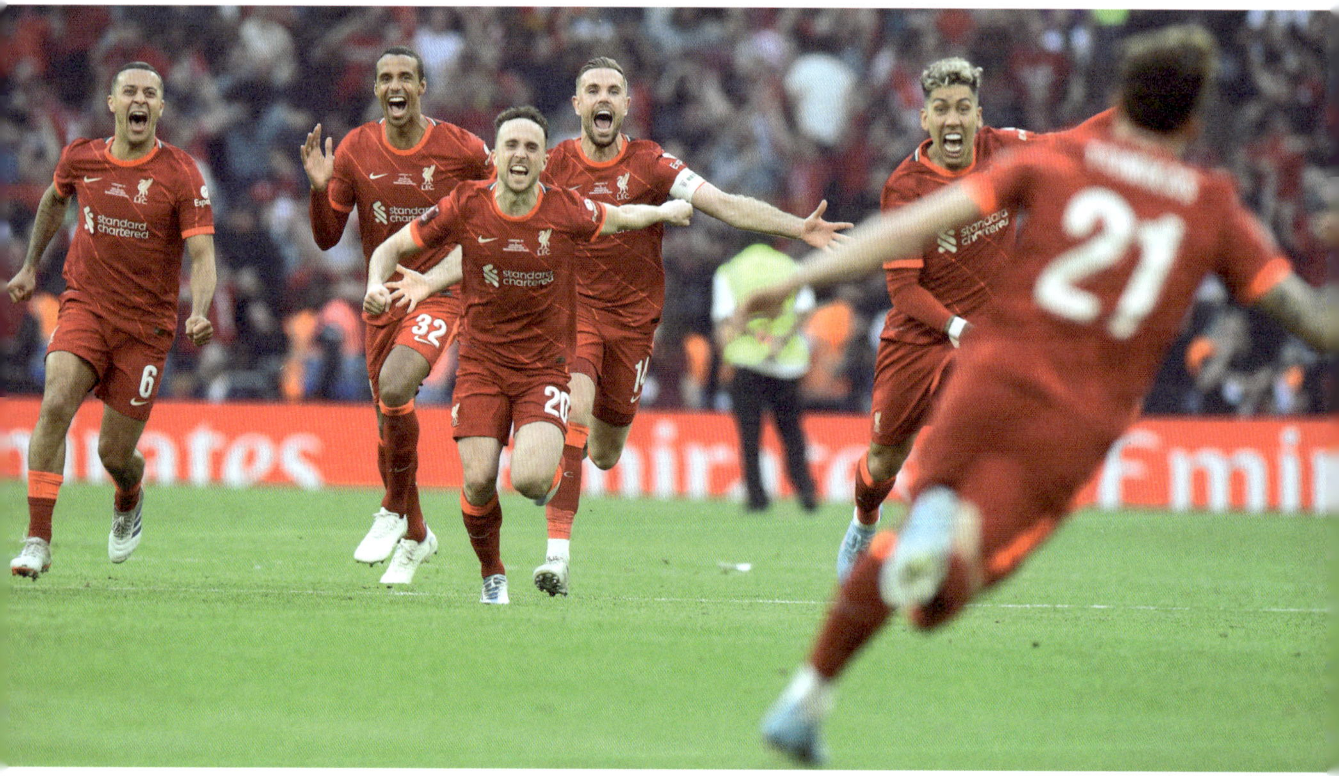
standard chartered
6
32
20

I FEEL FINE

LFC all-time honours:

League Champions: 1900/01, 1905/06, 1921/22, 1922/23, 1946/47, 1963/64, 1965/66, 1972/73, 1975/76, 1976/77, 1978/79, 1979/80, 1981/82, 1982/83, 1983/84, 1985/86, 1987/88, 1989/90, 2019/20 (19)

League Cup: 1901, 1982, 1983, 1984, 1995, 2001, 2003, 2012, 2022 (9)

FA Cup: 1965, 1974, 1986, 1989, 1992, 2001, 2006, 2022 (8)

European Cup: 1977, 1978, 1981, 1984, 2005, 2019 (6)

UEFA Super Cup: 1977, 2001, 2005, 2019 (4)

UEFA Cup: 1973, 1976, 2001 (3)

FIFA Club World Cup: 2019

93 ONE

One kiss is all it takes and one live performance from Dua Lipa was all it took for Liverpool supporters to be fallin' in love with her. The London-born singer was booked by UEFA to play the pre-match show ahead of the 2018 Champions League final in Kyiv. The headline tune of her set was One Kiss, a collaboration with Scottish DJ Calvin Harris released a month earlier. While Dua Lipa was doing her thing on the pitch inside the NSC Olimpiyskiy Stadium, travelling Kopites were singing along and dancing in the stands. It was a throwback to the 1960s, when Kopites would sing along to pre-match chart hits – including You'll Never Walk Alone – at Anfield while waiting for kick-off. Just two years earlier, at the 2016 UEFA Europa League final in Basel, Liverpool's travelling support had sung along to There She Goes by The La's at half-time, but there was something about One Kiss that stuck in Reds' minds. "One of the highlights of the night was definitely seeing the video of all the Liverpool fans

I FEEL FINE

chanting along to One Kiss afterwards – I felt very honoured," the three-time Grammy Award winner said in 2020. "I love Liverpool and it has always got a special place in my heart." In 2022, Liverpool players and supporters celebrated both the Carabao Cup and FA Cup final wins at Wembley by again singing along to One Kiss as it was blasted out over the PA system, footage of which was shared by both Dua Lipa and Calvin Harris on social media. After scoring the winning penalty against Chelsea in the FA Cup final, Kostas Tsimikas also admitted: "One Kiss is like motivation to celebrate more. I climbed on the back of Adrian. It was mad!" Later that month, red and white balloons were released from the roof when Dua Lipa performed One Kiss at the M&S Bank Arena – calling it "an unofficial anthem" – while Calvin Harris ended up DJing on Liverpool's open top bus tour of the city. "It was probably the biggest gig of my life," he said. One Kiss was all it took to make Dua Lipa an honorary Red.

94
THE CHAMPIONS WALL

When The Champions Wall was first installed in the reception area at Liverpool's old Melwood training ground in the summer of 2015 it had 44 major honours displayed upon it: 18 league titles, 5 European Cups, 7 FA Cups, 3 UEFA Cups, 8 League Cups and 3 UEFA Super Cups. Jürgen Klopp took charge of Liverpool FC in October 2015 and since then only the number of UEFA Cups hasn't needed updating with the silhouettes of two new trophies also added. Following the Reds' move from Melwood in 2020, The Champions Wall can now be found at both the AXA Training Centre and Anfield above a mosaic of legends, the Premier League trophy and FIFA Club World Cup proudly added at either end. It now features: 19 league titles, 6 European Cups, 8 FA Cups, 3 UEFA Cups, 9 League Cups, 4 UEFA Super Cups and 1 FIFA Club World Cup – a total of 50 major honours that makes Liverpool FC the most successful club in the history of English football. It is also a source of inspiration and motivation for Liverpool's players, with James Milner admitting in 2020: "I was desperate to get a trophy for this club – you walk into Melwood every day and you see the trophies the club has won every single day." Now Milly and his teammates can see many more. Six upgrades have been needed to The Champions Wall under Klopp's management and with the boss set to manage Liverpool until 2026, there may well be more to come.

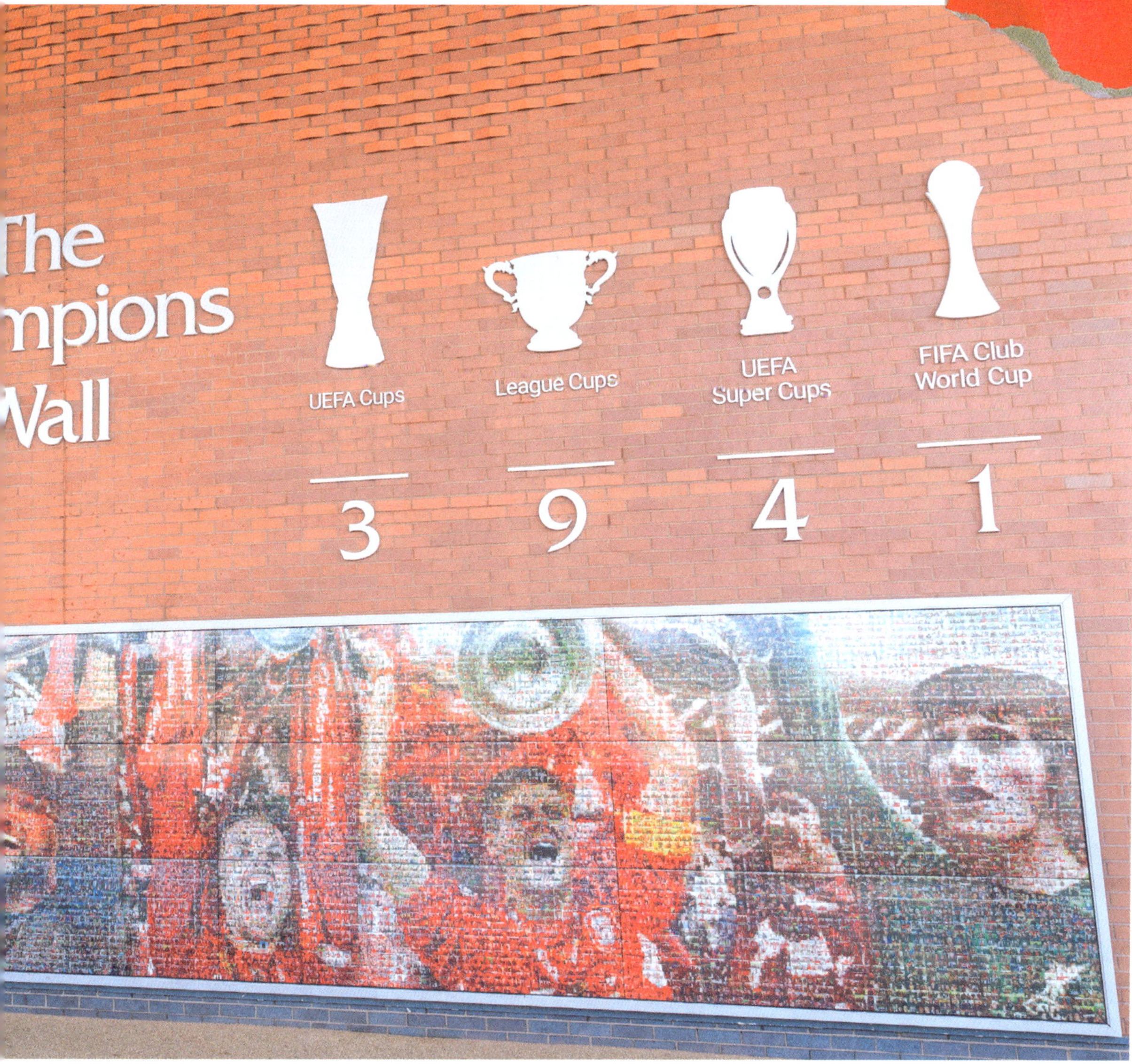
The
mpions
Wall
UEFA Cups
League Cups
UEFA
Super Cups
FIFA Club
World Cup
3
9
4
1

19

The Champions Wall
19
3
8
4
1

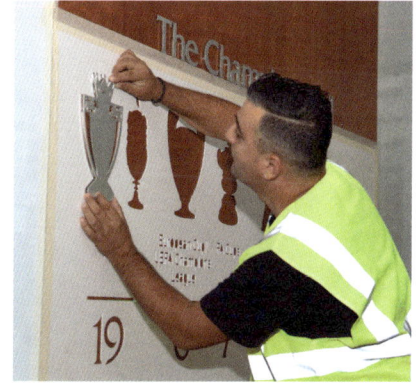

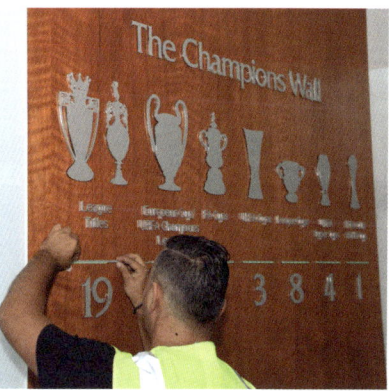

95
BEST STAFF IN THE BUSINESS

Bill Shankly's Bootroom was the most famous in football. Bob Paisley, Reuben Bennett, Joe Fagan, Ronnie Moran, Roy Evans, Tom Saunders and John Bennison underpinned Liverpool's success for three decades. The game is very different now, but having brilliant backroom staff is just as important. "I am nothing without my staff and what each member of the club brings to this project is what makes us what you see today," said Jürgen Klopp. The Liverpool manager's backroom staff totals around 30 people now from coaches, physios, masseurs and doctors to nutritionists, performance analysts and kit coordinators. Each play an integral role in LFC's collective success, but Klopp's two right-hand men – assistant managers Pep Lijnders and Peter Krawietz – are his closest confidants. In 2022 he admitted that their willingness to join him in signing new contracts was a key factor in persuading him to extend his stay as Liverpool boss and he spoke about both. "Pep and Pete's influence on our success and story together should not – and should never be – undervalued. What Pete sees on a football pitch is remarkable, really. I don't know how he does it, but

it's a talent and one that Liverpool FC are better for having. He is an outstanding and priceless coach. As for Pep, wow! I have been lucky enough to meet many, many people in football during my time in the game and I don't think I have ever met anyone with the energy and enthusiasm he has for this game. There is nothing he does not know about this sport. His passion for it is remarkable and his enthusiasm in training each day is infectious. I am the luckiest guy in the world to work with my players each day – and the same can be said of my staff. Not just Pep and Pete, but all the people at the AXA Training Centre who each day make such a big commitment to trying to make us the best we can possibly be. What you see on the pitch from the boys comes from the collective effort that's made each and every day here. We all share the same passion: to make Liverpool FC the best team and club in the world and that's really cool." Along with Vitor Matos, John Achterberg, Jack Robinson, Taffarel, Andreas Kornmayer, Mona Nemmer, Dr Andreas Schlumberger, Lee Nobes, Chris Morgan, Paul Small and many more, they're part of the best backroom staff in the business.

THE FULL SET

"Unreal, to be honest," replied Trent Alexander-Arnold when asked 'how does it feel to have lifted every major trophy as a Liverpool player by the age of 23?' "I was sitting there before the FA Cup final thinking 'this is the only one I've got left now to complete the set.'"

I FEEL FINE

"To do it is an amazing feeling. It's something that I've dreamed of and it's something that not many players can say they have done, so to be able to do it with this amazing club and this amazing team is a special feeling for me." To win the Champions League (2019), UEFA Super Cup (2019), FIFA Club World Cup (2019), Premier League (2020), League Cup (2022) and FA Cup (2022) by the age of 23 takes some doing and with the Reds having never previously lifted the FIFA Club World Cup, he's in the unique position of being the youngest player to complete the sextet of silverware with Liverpool. He's also won a Community Shield. Alexander-Arnold isn't the only member of Jürgen Klopp's squad to have won all six trophies – and skipper Jordan Henderson has two League Cup winners' medals having played in the Reds' 2012 final success as well – but for Trent to come through the Liverpool FC Academy and win the lot before his 24th birthday is a special achievement for a Scouser who grew up dreaming of lifting silverware for the club he adores.

> "I'M NOT REALLY THINKING ABOUT WHAT I'VE DONE, I'M MORE THINKING ABOUT WHAT I CAN DO, WHAT MORE I CAN ACHIEVE"
> – TRENT ALEXANDER-ARNOLD

97 SHIELD SUCCESS

Your view on the Community Shield usually hinges on whether your team has just won it or not. At the end of July 2022 many Reds were looking favourably on the honour, with Liverpool having just beaten perennial rivals Manchester City to strike a blow before the more serious stuff got going again. While the coaching staff might have seen this as a vital match to step up fitness and get more kilometres in squad members' legs, the boost the players received from earning the right for Jordan Henderson to get another trophy-lift shuffle in was obvious. It was also a chance for new signings to experience a showdown against a big Premier League opponent with a piece of silverware at stake. As it turned out, Jürgen Klopp resisted the temptation to start any of the new boys as Liverpool took a 1-0 half-time lead thanks to Trent Alexander-Arnold's slightly-deflected shot. Darwin Nunez was summoned from the bench just before the hour-mark, but it was City debutant Julian Alvarez that struck next to equalise. Into the final 10 minutes the Reds were awarded a penalty as Nunez's header was handled by Ruben Dias, allowing the pin-sharp Mo Salah to fire home from 12 yards. Fabio Carvalho came on with a few minutes to go and had a close-up view as Nunez rounded off a lively first game at the King Power Stadium by nodding in to make it 3-1. It was the first time a Liverpool player had scored on debut since Virgil van Dijk in 2018 and ensured Klopp had won the Community Shield for the first time.

I FEEL FINE

I FEEL FINE

Most recent 10 players to score on their Liverpool FC debut

Darwin Nunez	v Manchester City	Community Shield	30.07.22
Virgil van Dijk	v Everton	FA Cup	05.01.18
Mohamed Salah	v Watford	Premier League	12.08.17
Sadio Mane	v Arsenal	Premier League	14.08.16
Jordan Rossiter	v Middlesbrough	League Cup	23.09.14
Victor Moses	v Swansea City	Premier League	16.09.13
Daniel Sturridge	v Mansfield Town	FA Cup	06.01.13
Andre Wisdom	v Young Boys	Europa League	20.09.12
Luis Suarez	v Stoke City	Premier League	02.02.11
Gabriel Paletta	v Reading	League Cup	25.10.06

I FEEL FINE

RECORD BREAKERS 98

You have to really go some to break records at a club with a history as successful as Liverpool FC's, but the Reds' recent crop, under the guidance of an inspirational manager, have managed to set new benchmarks. It's difficult to list them all, but here are a selection of club and player records that have been set under Jürgen Klopp…

99 points
The most points the Reds have ever accumulated in a league season is 99, set when they won the Premier League in 2019/20. The season before they reached 97 points but, remarkably, it wasn't enough to claim the title.

12 wins in a row
The highest number of games Liverpool have ever won in a row in all competitions is 12, set between 16 January and 5 March 2022.

50 not out
In September 2019 Sadio Mane became the first player in Premier League history to reach 50 home appearances with one club without defeat [41 wins, nine draws].

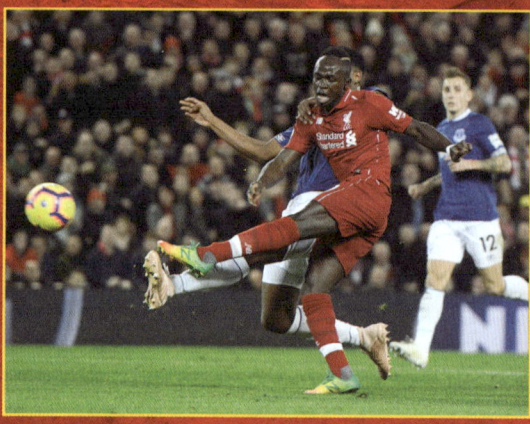

Quick wins
The 5-2 win over Everton in December 2019 saw Jürgen Klopp reach 100 league wins faster than any manager in Liverpool FC history.

I FEEL FINE

Best start
After beating Tottenham in January 2020 to make it 20 victories in their first 21 league games, the Reds set the record for the best ever start to a top-flight season in Europe's top five leagues. They stretched that record to 26 wins in 27 games.

Relentless
The 2019/20 season saw the Reds become the fastest team to reach 30 league wins in a single season (34 matches).

Beating everyone
When they beat West Ham in January 2020, the Reds had beaten every other team in the top flight in a single season for the first time.

Whopping points tally
Following the 3-2 win against West Ham in February 2020, the Reds had accumulated a record 110 points in a 38-game stretch – continuing from the end of the 2018/19 season.

Mo's openers
Mohamed Salah is the first player in Premier League history to score a goal in the opening game of the season six times in succession.

Double treble
Bobby Firmino became the first Brazilian to net two Premier League hat-tricks after his treble at Watford in 2021.

Champions haul
Mo Salah is the Reds' top goalscorer of all-time in the Champions League with 34 goals.

Records tumble at Old Trafford
When Liverpool beat Manchester United at Old Trafford 5-0 in October 2021, they became the first English top-flight team to score three or more times in nine consecutive away matches in all competitions. Having also beaten Watford 5-0, Liverpool won consecutive league games by 5+ goals for the first time since 1935 when they beat Stoke 5-0 and Chelsea 6-0. Mo Salah became the first opposition player to score a Premier League hat-trick at Old Trafford as he also completed his 10th consecutive goalscoring game for the Reds.

I FEEL FINE

Hungry for goals
A 4-1 win at Goodison Park in December 2021 meant the Reds had scored two or more goals in a record 18 successive matches.

Hit for six
A win against AC Milan at the San Siro in December 2021 meant Liverpool FC became the first English team to win all six Champions League group games in one campaign.

MORE 2019/20 FACTS

– AT ONE STAGE THE REDS HAD A **25**-POINT LEAD AT THE TOP OF THE PREMIER LEAGUE, THE BIGGEST EVER LEAD IN THE ENGLISH TOP-FLIGHT

– LIVERPOOL FC WON THE PREMIER LEAGUE WITH **SEVEN** GAMES TO SPARE – THE EARLIEST THE TITLE HAD EVER BEEN WON

– **14** AWAY LEAGUE WINS IS THE MOST THE CLUB HAVE EVER ACHIEVED IN ONE SEASON

– FOR THE FIRST TIME, LIVERPOOL FC REMAINED UNBEATEN IN THE LEAGUE AT ANFIELD FOR A **THIRD** CONSECUTIVE SEASON

– THE REDS EARNED **13** LEAGUE DOUBLES IN A SEASON FOR THE FIRST TIME

Rush hour
Mo Salah is the first Liverpool FC player since Ian Rush to score 20 or more goals in five successive seasons.

Half-century
In their 18th Premier League match of the 2021/22 season, the Reds reached 50 goals – the fewest number of games they have taken to reach that landmark.

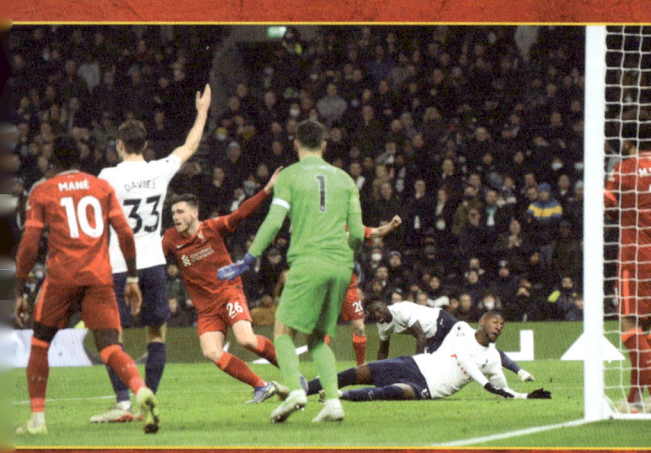

Young Harvey
In February 2022, Harvey Elliott became the youngest player to start a Champions League game for the Reds, aged 18 years and 318 days, against Inter Milan at the San Siro.

United undone
A 4-0 win at Anfield in April 2022 meant the Reds became the first team in the Premier League era to score at least eight goals against Manchester United in one season following the 5-0 win at Old Trafford in October. Mo Salah's double meant he became the first Liverpool player to score five league goals against Manchester United in a single season.

Not-so-young Milly
At the age of 36, James Milner became the oldest Englishman to start a Champions League match when he did so against Benfica in April 2022.

Sub-stantial contribution
Divock Origi's final goal for the Reds, in a 2-0 win over Everton in April 2022, was his 11th goal as a substitute in the Premier League, more than any other Liverpool FC player.

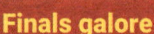

Finals galore
In 2022 the Reds became the first English club to reach the final of the European Cup, FA Cup and League Cup in the same season. Jürgen Klopp became the fourth manager to reach four European Cup finals after Marcello Lippi, Alex Ferguson and Carlo Ancelotti.

I FEEL FINE

Hitting a maximum
147 goals in the 2021/22 season is a record for a single season for the Reds.

Captain fantastic
Jordan Henderson is the first Englishman to captain a team in three different Champions League finals.

CONSECUTIVE RESULTS…

– RECORD CONSECUTIVE LEAGUE WINS: 18 (FROM 27 OCTOBER 2019 TO 24 FEBRUARY 2020)

– RECORD CONSECUTIVE LEAGUE MATCHES WITHOUT A DEFEAT: 44 (FROM 12 JANUARY 2019 TO 24 FEBRUARY 2020)

– RECORD CONSECUTIVE HOME LEAGUE WINS: 24 (FROM 9 FEBRUARY 2019 TO 5 JULY 2020)

– RECORD CONSECUTIVE HOME LEAGUE MATCHES WITHOUT DEFEAT: 68 (FROM 7 MAY 2017 TO 17 JANUARY 2021)

Scoring almost every game
Mo Salah holds the club record for the most goalscoring games during a single campaign with 34 (2017/18).

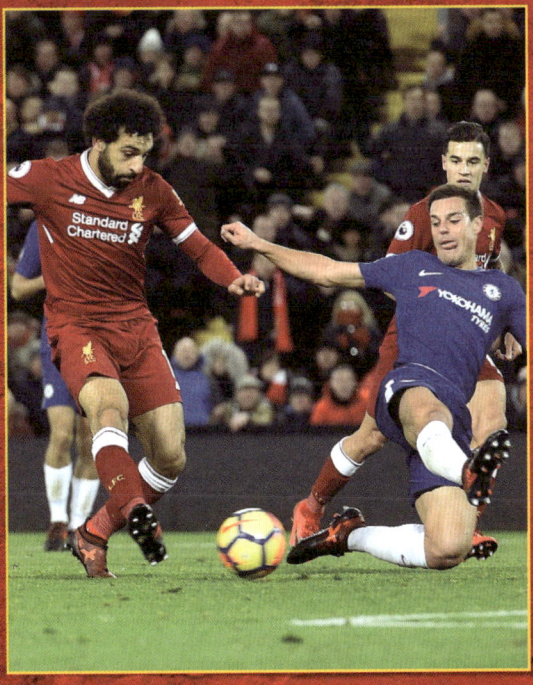

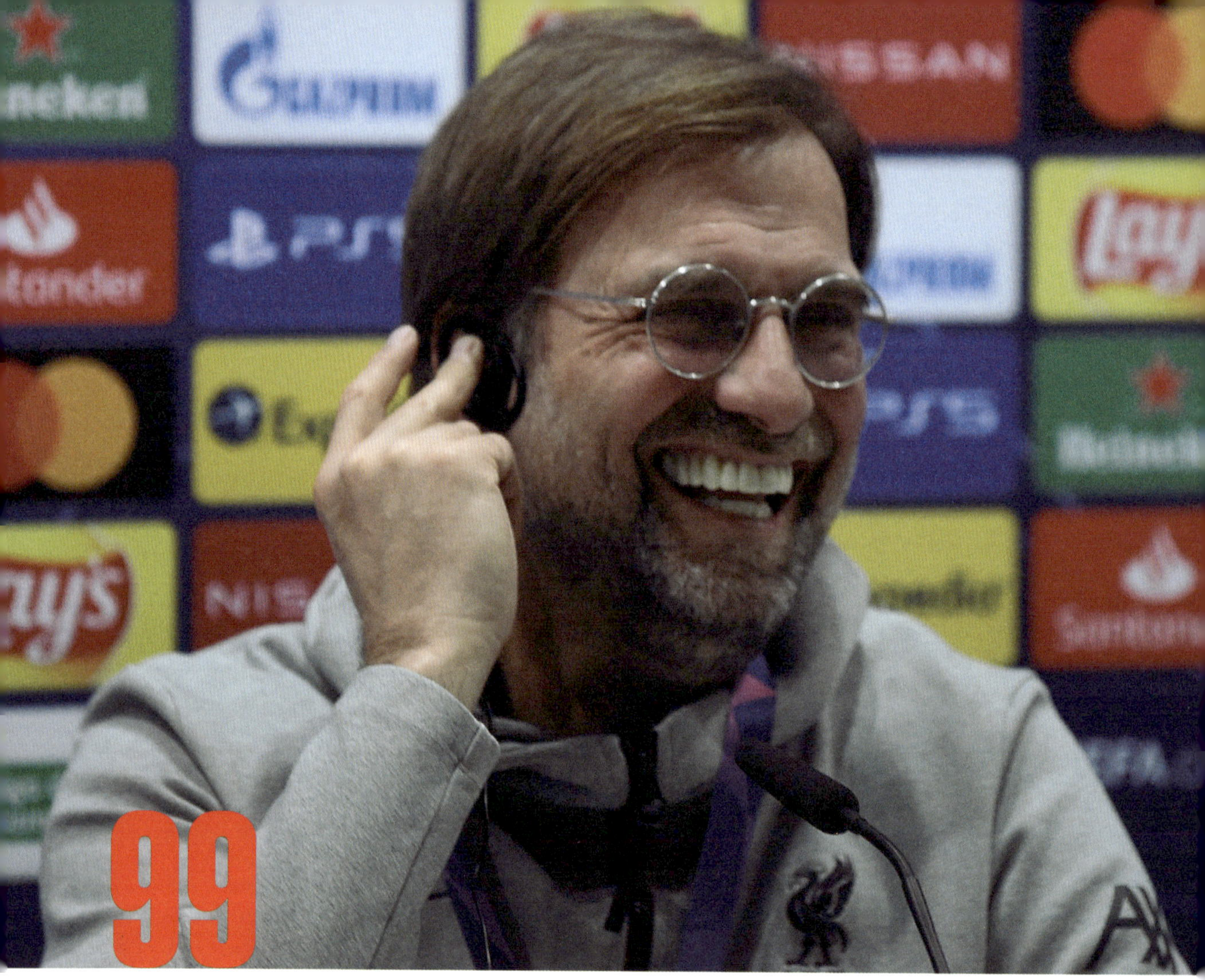

99
NEVER LOST FOR WORDS

Picking a selection of interesting, thoughtful or amusing quotes from Jürgen Klopp is like identifying a few favourite grains of sand on a beach. There are just so many to choose from. When the boss isn't working with his players, he's often conducting interviews. Here are just a few of the things he's had to say over the years...

I FEEL FINE

Philosophy

"I heard from my agent that Liverpool is interested and I felt it's like when I met my wife – I saw her and thought 'okay, I'll marry her', and it was like that with this club. It felt right from the first moment"

"WE WANT TO ATTACK THE OPPONENT NON-STOP WHEN WE HAVE THE BALL, WHEN WE LOSE IT, AND WHEN THE OPPOSITION HAVE IT. PUT ANOTHER WAY, DEFENDING IS OUR FIRST OFFENSIVE ACTION"

"GIVING ABSOLUTELY EVERYTHING DOESN'T MEAN YOU GET ANYTHING BUT IT'S THE ONLY CHANCE TO GET SOMETHING"

"LIVERPOOL IS A CLUB WITH A BIG, BIG, BIG HISTORY, AND ALL THE CLUBS IN THE WORLD HAVE A BIG HISTORY IF THE PRESENT IS NOT TOO SUCCESSFUL. IF YOU HAVE NEVER HAD SUCCESS, NOBODY KNOWS HOW IT IS, BUT IN LIVERPOOL, EVERYBODY KNOWS HOW IT WAS"

I FEEL FINE

His players

"WITHOUT PLAYERS LIKE JAMES MILNER, SUCCESS IN FOOTBALL IS PRETTY MUCH IMPOSSIBLE"

"WHEN YOU THINK OF MO SALAH, YOU THINK ABOUT AN OUTSTANDING FOOTBALLER AND A GREAT GOALSCORER, WHAT YOU MAY NOT SEE IS WHAT KIND OF A GOOD PERSON HE IS. IF I TELL YOU HE IS AN EVEN BETTER PERSON THAN HE IS A PLAYER, THEN YOU CAN IMAGINE WHAT TYPE OF A GUY HE IS"

"THOSE WITH FOOTBALL KNOWLEDGE KNOW HOW IMPORTANT HE IS [BOBBY FIRMINO]. I'M PRETTY SURE PEOPLE WILL WRITE BOOKS ABOUT HOW HE INTERPRETED THE FALSE NINE POSITION. I WON'T SAY HE INVENTED IT, BUT THE WAY HE PLAYS IT, IT LOOKS LIKE IT!"

"IF ANYONE SAYS THAT TRENT CANNOT DEFEND THEN THEY CAN COME TO ME AND I'LL KNOCK THEM DOWN. I CANNOT HEAR THAT ANY MORE, I DON'T KNOW WHAT MORE THE BOY HAS TO DO"

"I NEVER WANT TO GIVE HIM [JORDAN HENDERSON] THE FEELING HE HAS A POINT TO PROVE BECAUSE I KNOW HIS NATURAL MOTIVATION IS ALREADY AT THE LIMIT SO YOU DON'T HAVE TO PUT OIL IN THE FIRE. THERE'S ENOUGH FIRE THERE ALREADY. THAT'S HENDO"

Humour

"I'VE MET SOME EVERTONIANS IN THE STREET AND THEY'VE BEEN FRIENDLY. I'VE HAD TAXI DRIVERS WHO HAVE BEEN EVERTON FANS. THEY'VE BEEN REALLY NICE. AT THE BEGINNING I THOUGHT 'OKAY, MAYBE THEY'RE HAPPY I'M HERE BECAUSE THEY THINK THAT MEANS LIVERPOOL WON'T HAVE ANY SUCCESS FOR THE NEXT 20 YEARS!'"

[On playing behind closed doors]
"WHEN I WAS A PLAYER WE PLAYED IN EMPTY STADIUMS AND THERE WERE NO BANS. THEY JUST WEREN'T INTERESTED IN THE FOOTBALL WE PLAYED!"

[On English fans compared to those in Germany]
"IT'S MORE INTENSE. IT'S MORE IMPORTANT FOR THE PEOPLE IF YOU ARE WINNING OR NOT – PROBABLY BECAUSE YOU ENGLISH PEOPLE BET MUCH MORE!"

"I DON'T THINK I CAN COACH IN ITALY. THE ONLY THING I CAN SAY IN ITALIAN IS TO ORDER A PLATE OF SPAGHETTI"

[On the voice of a translator in his earpiece]
"THAT'S A VERY EROTIC VOICE BY THE WAY…CONGRATULATIONS…WOW…AGAIN PLEASE!"

[On arriving in Bangkok for a pre-season match against Manchester United]
"THE FIRST QUESTION I HAVE IS: DID IT LOOK LIKE THIS [BUSY] YESTERDAY WHEN MANCHESTER [UNITED] WAS HERE?"

[After Mo Salah won the PFA Player Of The Year award]
"FROM THE LFC FAMILY, CONGRATULATIONS. BUT NOW, GRAB THE TROPHY AND RUN HOME…WE PLAY ON TUESDAY"

"IT'S NORMAL THAT PEOPLE ARE POSITIVE ABOUT THE MANAGER WHEN YOU BECOME CHAMPIONS BUT THE PEOPLE KNOW AS WELL THAT I KNOW HOW MUCH IT MEANS. I AM THE FACE OF IT BUT A LOT OF THE WORK MY STAFF DO AND THAT'S HOW IT IS"

[After the parade following the 2019 Champions League win]

"I CANNOT REALLY DESCRIBE IT BECAUSE I CRIED A LITTLE BIT AS WELL BECAUSE IT'S SO OVERWHELMING WHAT THE PEOPLE ARE DOING. WHEN YOU HAVE DIRECT EYE CONTACT AND YOU SEE HOW MUCH IT MEANS TO THEM, THAT'S TOUCHING, TO BE HONEST. IT'S BRILLIANT"

I FEEL FINE

Success

[After the famous Barcelona semi-final in 2019]
"WE KNOW THIS CLUB IS A MIX OF ATMOSPHERE, EMOTION, DESIRE AND FOOTBALL QUALITY. CUT OFF ONE AND IT DOESN'T WORK – WE KNOW THAT. I'VE SAID IT BEFORE. IF I HAVE TO DESCRIBE THIS CLUB THEN IT'S A BIG HEART AND TONIGHT IT WAS OBVIOUSLY LIKE CRAZY, POUNDING LIKE CRAZY. YOU COULD HEAR IT AND PROBABLY FEEL IT ALL OVER THE WORLD"

[On making sure Liverpool play Champions League football]
"I THINK IN THE LAST 10 YEARS LIVERPOOL WAS NOT PART OF IT TOO OFTEN. WE SHOULD TRY EVERYTHING TO CHANGE THIS, WE HAVE TO MAKE STEPS AND THE STEP FOR US IS TO BE AROUND THE BEST TEAMS IN THE WORLD BECAUSE WE ARE ONE OF THE BEST CLUBS"

[2019 Champions League final]
"I FEEL MOSTLY RELIEVED. RELIEF FOR MY FAMILY ACTUALLY, BECAUSE THEY ARE PRETTY CLOSE TO ME AND THE LAST SIX TIMES [IN FINALS] WE ALWAYS FLEW ON HOLIDAY WITH A SILVER MEDAL THAT DOESN'T FEEL TOO COOL – AND THIS IS COMPLETELY DIFFERENT THIS YEAR SO IT'S FOR THEM AS WELL"

[2022 FA Cup final]
"I CAN SAY WHATEVER I WANT, I CAN MOTIVATE AS MUCH AS I WANT, [BUT] IF THESE BOYS DON'T LISTEN, IF THESE BOYS ARE A LITTLE BIT DISTRACTED BY WHATEVER OR GET WEAK OR SOFT OR WHATEVER, THEN IN THIS MOMENT YOU DON'T HAVE A CHANCE… BUT TODAY IS THE FA CUP AND WE WON THE GAME AND WE HAVE THE MEDAL, A WONDERFUL T-SHIRT. THAT'S ENOUGH FOR THE MOMENT"

I FEEL FINE

A full stadium, motivation… and staying put!

[AFTER THE RETURN OF FANS AND A FULL ANFIELD FOR THE VISIT OF BURNLEY IN 2021]
"EVERYBODY WAS REALLY LOOKING FORWARD TO THIS FOOTBALL FESTIVAL, TO THIS GAME, AND I THINK NOBODY LEAVES THIS PLACE TODAY WITH ANY KIND OF DISAPPOINTMENT BECAUSE I THINK ALL OF OUR DREAMS WERE FULFILLED TODAY, ATMOSPHERE-WISE"

I FEEL FINE

[On defeat to Sevilla in the 2016 Europa League final in Basel]
"WE WILL USE THIS EXPERIENCE TOGETHER. THEN SOME DAY EVERYBODY WILL SAY BASEL WAS A VERY DECISIVE MOMENT FOR THE WONDERFUL FUTURE OF LIVERPOOL FC"

[On signing a new contract]
"WHEN THE OWNERS BROUGHT THE POSSIBILITY TO RENEW TO ME, I ASKED MYSELF THE QUESTION I'VE MUSED OVER PUBLICLY. DO I HAVE THE ENERGY AND VIBE TO GIVE OF MYSELF AGAIN WHAT THIS AMAZING PLACE REQUIRES FROM THE PERSON IN THE MANAGER'S OFFICE? I DIDN'T NEED TOO LONG TO ANSWER IN TRUTH. THE ANSWER WAS VERY SIMPLE… I'M IN LOVE WITH HERE AND I FEEL FINE!"

"I'M IN LOVE WITH HIM AND I FEEL FINE"

It is often in the knock-out stages of European competition when new Liverpool songs emerge as excitement builds among supporters about the possibility of the Reds winning silverware. Lisbon 2022 will be remembered for the arrival of an absolute banger. "Jürgen said to me, you know, we'll win the Premier League, you know, he said so. I'm in love with him and I feel fine. I'm so glad that Jürgen is a Red, I'm so glad he delivered what he said. Jürgen said to me, you know, we'll win the Premier League, you know, he said so. I'm in love with him and I feel fine." Previously, in their desire to innovate, Kopites had largely shied away from doing the obvious and reworking songs by The Beatles as a signature tune, but this was a throwback to the glory days of the 1960s celebrating a Premier League title win in the 2020s. When this new version of I Feel Fine did the rounds in a Lisbon bar and hit social media ahead of the Champions League quarter-final first leg against Benfica it went viral. The Reds beat Benfica 3-1 in Estadio da Luz, Luis Diaz netting his first European goal for Liverpool, but the 'new Klopp song' was an earworm. When the second leg followed at Anfield a week later it rang out throughout the night and the sound of I Feel Fine echoing around Wembley during the FA Cup semi-final and final wins against Manchester City and Chelsea left us in no doubt that it was the song of an incredible season. Maybe it should have been updated by Kopites in August 2022 when Liverpool equalled both the Premier League record win and club-record home league win with a stunning 9-0 success against Bournemouth. I'm in love with him and I feel NINE would have been quite apt that afternoon. Jürgen Klopp may not be the most comfortable person hearing his name sung, much preferring the adulation to go to his players, but Liverpool's longest-serving manager since Bob Paisley deserves a song of such stature because, quite simply, we're all so glad that Jürgen is a Red.